CORNWALL

Sketchbook
A pictorial guide to favourite coastal places

Jim Watson

Thatched Cottage, Sennen Cove

SURVIVAL BOOKS • BATH • ENGLAND

The Old Watch House, Polperro

First published 2012

Survival Books Limited
Office 169, 3 Edgar Buildings,
George Street, Bath BA1 2FJ, United Kingdom
Tel: +44 (0)1935-700060
email: sales@survivalbooks.net
website: www.survivalbooks.net

British Library Cataloguing in Publication Data
ACIP record for this book is available
from the British Library.
ISBN: 978-1-907339-41-7

Front cover illustration: St Ives harbour   Printed and bound in Malaysia by Tien Wah Press

CONTENTS

Approaching Zennor on the
B3306 St Ives to St Just road

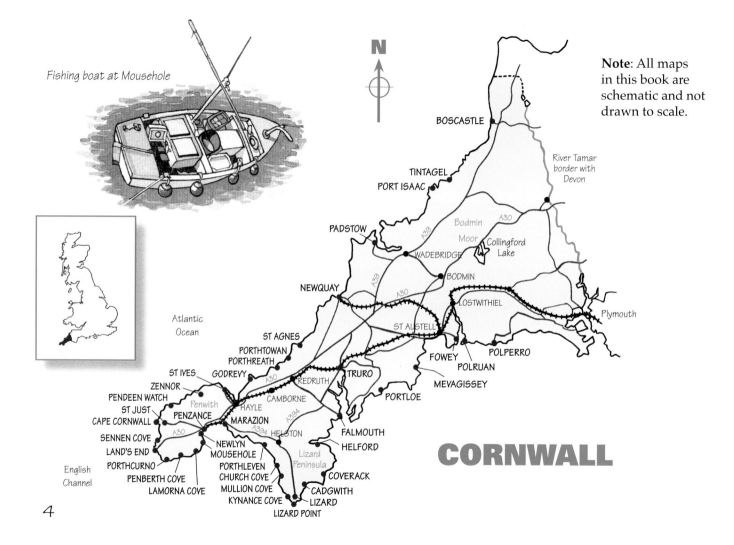

Fishing boat at Mousehole

N

BOSCASTLE

River Tamar border with Devon

TINTAGEL

PORT ISAAC

PADSTOW

Bodmin Moor

Collingford Lake

A30

WADEBRIDGE

A39

BODMIN

NEWQUAY

A39

A30

LOSTWITHIEL

Plymouth

ST AUSTELL

Atlantic Ocean

ST AGNES

PORTHTOWAN

PORTHREATH

FOWEY

POLPERRO

POLRUAN

ST IVES

GODREVY

A30

REDRUTH

TRURO

MEVAGISSEY

ZENNOR

Penwith

CAMBORNE

PENDEEN WATCH

HAYLE

ST JUST

PENZANCE

PORTLOE

CAPE CORNWALL

MARAZION

A394

SENNEN COVE

A30

HELSTON

FALMOUTH

LAND'S END

NEWLYN

A394

HELFORD

PORTHCURNO

MOUSEHOLE

Lizard Peninsula

English Channel

PENBERTH COVE

PORTHLEVEN

CHURCH COVE

COVERACK

LAMORNA COVE

MULLION COVE

CADGWITH

KYNANCE COVE

LIZARD

LIZARD POINT

CORNWALL

INTRODUCTION

For me, Cornwall has it all: beauty, drama, serenity and inspiration. There's also a timeless, unchanging quality that has sustained me for the more than 40 years I've been enjoying its cliffs, beaches and villages.

Cornwall makes up the western tip of a long arm of land thrusting into the Atlantic Ocean, as though it wants to escape from the rest of England. Indeed, it's separated from Devon – and England – for most of its length by the River Tamar, with only a seven-mile stretch of land keeping it from breaking free. This separateness also extends to the Cornish culture, which has retained its Celtic heritage and is rich in myth and legend, a place of standing stones, Gothic tales and smuggling sagas.

There are plenty of places inland that are worth visiting but it's the fabulous coastline that most of us flock to. Cornwall has the longest and most diverse coastline in Britain. Depending on how it's measured, headland to headland or water's edge, it stretches 300 or just over 1,000 miles. At its broadest, the county is only around 45 miles wide, so you're never more than 25 miles from the sea. It has over 300 beaches and 12 separate Areas of Outstanding Natural Beauty.

This book will guide you to a plethora of favourite places, a journey beginning at Boscastle in the northwest, rounding Land's End and ending at Polperro in the southeast. It shows you how to get there – with detailed maps – where you can park and what to look out for. There are also some easy walks. The South West Coast Path follows the entire Cornish coastline, so if you join at any point you're guaranteed a well-maintained and waymarked route with fabulous views.

This book is a celebration, but I also hope it informs and entertains. Producing it has been a pleasure, a journey of discovery and most of all, a labour of love. These are some of my favourite places – anywhere. I hope they give you as much pleasure as they always give me.

Jim Watson

Rugby, 2012

Splendid isolation – a seaside home at Coverack

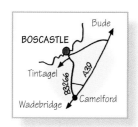

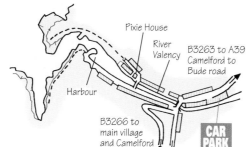

Pixie House

River Valency

B3263 to A39 Camelford to Bude road

Harbour

B3266 to main village and Camelford

CAR PARK

The main village of Boscastle sits grandly up the hillside, leaving the harbour at the bottom to conduct the business of tourism with avid vigour.

It was once a significant port, the only one for 20 miles, as well as a fishing harbour. The fishing boats struggle on but Boscastle is now given over almost entirely to its visitors.

BOSCASTLE

The 300 year-old Pixie House (the Harbour Light), famous for its crooked roof, was reputedly the most photographed building in Boscastle.

However, in 2004 it took the full brunt of the floods and was completely destroyed. Within two years it was returned to its former glory, rebuilt with every nook and cranny carefully recreated.

The rebuilt Pixie House

Boscastle from the harbour

On August 16, 2004, torrential rain pounded Boscastle for eight hours, increasing river levels by 7ft (2m) in a single hour. The River Valency burst its banks, sending 440 million gallons of water cascading down the main street at up to 40 miles an hour, uprooting trees, washing away boulders and, ultimately, buildings.

The torrent picked up vehicles in the car park and a surreal procession of small cars and camper vans was captured on camera, and witnessed on television around the world. Some 75 cars, 5 caravans, 6 buildings and several boats were washed into the sea; approximately 100 homes and businesses were destroyed; trees were uprooted and debris scattered over a large area. In an operation lasting from mid-afternoon until 2.30am, a fleet of 7 helicopters rescued around 150 people clinging to trees and the roofs of buildings and cars. Remarkably, no major injuries or loss of life occurred.

With commendable urgency, the people of Boscastle set about rebuilding their community. Within a couple years businesses were up and running again and there's few signs these days of the devastation. Cynics might say the rebuilding has turned a tourist set piece into even more of a stage set, but the tourists who flock to the undeniably picturesque harbour don't seem to mind too much.

The harbour

The harbour exit to the sea

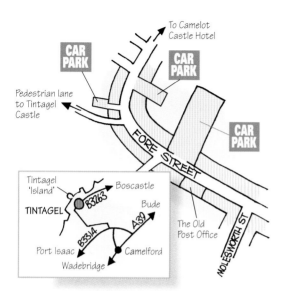

To Camelot Castle Hotel

CAR PARK

CAR PARK

Pedestrian lane to Tintagel Castle

CAR PARK

FORE STREET

Tintagel 'Island'
B3263
Boscastle
TINTAGEL
Bude
A39
B3314
Port Isaac
Camelford
Wadebridge

The Old Post Office

NOLESWORTH ST

King Arthur Bookshop

Fore Street and the lane to the castle, with an inevitably-named bookshop

The Old Post Office

TINTAGEL

Unusually for Cornish tourist centres (at least in this book) this one straddles a hilltop rather than being snuggled down in a cove with its feet in the sea. Tintagel is a long straggly village with no obvious reason for being there except as an adjunct to a castle, a function it continues to perform admirably to this day.

The modern-day village was known as 'Trevena' until the Post Office established 'Tintagel' in the mid-19th century. Before then 'Tintagel' had been the name of the headland and the parish.

Appropriately, the village's premier attraction is the 'Old Post Office', which dates from the 14th century. The charismatic, grey-stone manor house, which became a post office during the 19th century, is now Grade I listed and owned by the National Trust. It attracts more than 45,000 visitors a year and is handily positioned just across the road from an expansive car and coach park.

8

A half-mile west of the village, Tintagel Island is connected to the mainland by a narrow neck of land facing the full force of the Atlantic. A place of settlement, mystery and extreme weather since Roman times, it was always well qualified to take on the mantle of the Arthurian myth.

The legend began in the 12th century when Geoffrey of Monmouth published his mythical history of Britain, describing Tintagel as the place of Arthur's conception. During the 13th century, Richard, Earl of Cornwall, was so inspired by the tale that he built a castle on the 'island' peninsula in a deliberate old-fashioned style to make it look more ancient. This eventually fell into ruin and is largely what we see today.

The castle features in the doomed romance of Tristan and Isolde, the inspiration for Wagner's epic opera. Victorians flocked here after the Arthurian connection was revitalised in poetry by Alfred, Lord Tennyson and others.

The ruins are breathtaking. Steep stone steps, stout walls and rugged windswept cliff edges encircle the great hall, where Richard, Earl of Cornwall, once feasted. The views are sensational and when sea mist suddenly swirls around the ramparts on a sunny day, myth and magic become a powerful possibility.

The ruins of the upper mainland courtyards

Camelot Castle Hotel   Tintagel village

The rugged coastline from the castle

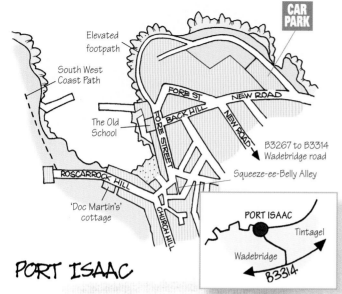

Elevated footpath

South West Coast Path

CAR PARK

FORE ST

NEW ROAD

NEW ROAD

The Old School

ROSCARROCK HILL

BACK HILL

FORE STREET

CHURCH HILL

'Doc Martin's' cottage

B3267 to B3314 Wadebridge road

Squeeze-ee-Belly Alley

PORT ISAAC

Tintagel

Wadebridge

B3314

PORT ISAAC

The Platt

Fore Street

For many years visitors knew Port Isaac as 'the place you park on the beach'. These days that facility seems to come and go but as the narrow twisting streets of the village are no place for modern vehicles, the large car park at the top of the hill is the best option. The footpath around the cliff top is a superb viewpoint, and the stroll down Fore Street through an avenue of picturesque cottages and interesting shops is a delight.

The Platt, a small square and stoney beach at the bottom of the hill, is usually a chaotic scene of fishing paraphernalia, squawking seagulls, lounging tourists, bendy buildings and a welcoming old pub with it's doors flung open. The perfect Cornish holiday scene. It can be sunny too!

Port Isaac has been a fishing village since the 14th century. The pier was constructed during the reign of Henry VIII. The village's central area dates from the 18th and 19th centuries, from a time when its prosperity was tied to local coastal freight and fishing. The port handled cargoes such as coal, timber, salt, pottery, stone and Delabole slate from nearby quarries, which were conveyed down its narrow streets. With the construction of the North Cornwall Railway in 1895 and a station – Port Isaac Road – built three miles from the village, transport trade in the tiny port was effectively killed off and Port Isaac became dependent mainly on fishing. Fishermen still work from the Platt, landing a daily catch of fish, crab and lobsters. Port Isaac Road station closed in 1966.

Port Isaac's narrow, winding streets are lined with old white-washed cottages and traditional granite, slate-fronted Cornish houses, many of which are listed as of architectural or historic importance. It's a wonderful place to explore, just picking a street at random and seeing where it takes you.

Squeeze-ee-Belly Alley measures just nineteen and a half inches wide, officially the narrowest of such alley-ways, certified by the *Guiness Book of Records*

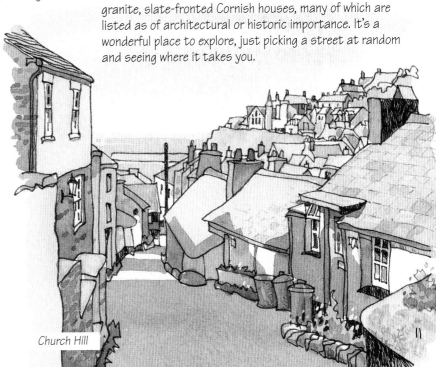

A hidden-away corner

Church Hill

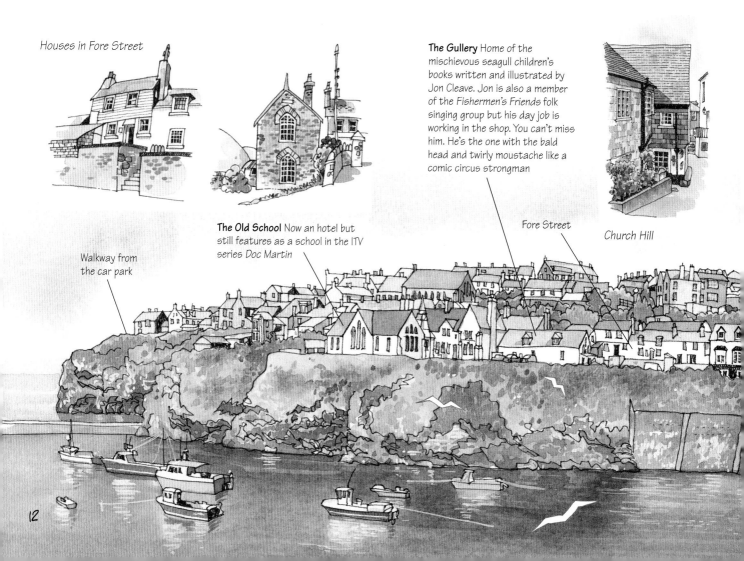

Houses in Fore Street

The Old School Now an hotel but still features as a school in the ITV series *Doc Martin*

The Gullery Home of the mischievous seagull children's books written and illustrated by Jon Cleave. Jon is also a member of the Fishermen's Friends folk singing group but his day job is working in the shop. You can't miss him. He's the one with the bald head and twirly moustache like a comic circus strongman

Fore Street

Church Hill

Walkway from the car park

12

Port Isaac is home to the *Fisherman's Friends*, a group of sea shanty singers who perform on summer Friday evenings on the Platt outside the pub. If wet, in the pub. In 2010 they signed an album deal for £1 million with Universal. The group is made up of ten local men who live in the village and grew up together. It includes fishermen, farmers and shopkeepers. One is in his seventies. As Port Isaac's Fisherman's Friends they have performed all over the UK, including the Royal Albert Hall, and have appeared on the popular television quiz show *Eggheads*.

The village is a popular venue for film and TV shoots. Films include *Saving Grace* and *Nightmare Man* - where Port Isaac was depicted as the Hebrides. The TV series *Poldark* was filmed here and more recently it became Port Wenn for ITV's *Doc Martin* starring Martin Clunes as the irascible GP.

Port Isaac is always a pleasure to visit and the demands of tourism don't seem to have overwhelmed its community spirit. Long may it continue.

The Golden Lion A splendid old pub with a dark smuggling history. Great place for a banter, a crab sandwich and a pint

The Platt

Port Isaac from Roscarrock Hill

13

The Camel estuary cuts deeply into the north Cornwall coastline, so to cross from one side to the other requires a road trip of around 15 miles via Wadebridge. Consequently there have been ferries across the Camel for centuries. The current service carries foot passengers between Padstow and Rock daily.

Traditionally a fishing port, Padstow is now a popular tourist destination. Although some of its former fishing fleet remains, it's mainly a yachting haven on a dramatic coastline with few easily navigable harbours.

The celebrity chef and restaurateur, Rick Stein, has had a considerable influence on Padstow. He now has five eateries in the town and tourists travel from far away to eat at his restaurant and cafés.

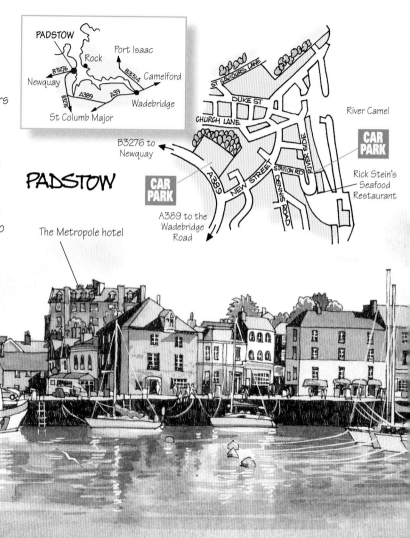

PADSTOW

PADSTOW
Rock
Port Isaac
Newquay
B3276
Camelford
B3314
A389
A39
Wadebridge
St Columb Major

River Camel

CAR PARK

B3276 to Newquay

PADSTOW

CAR PARK

Rick Stein's Seafood Restaurant

A389 to the Wadebridge Road

ST SAVIOURS LANE
DUKE ST
CHURCH LANE
NEW STREET
STATION RD
RIVER SIDE
DENNIS ROAD
A389

The Metropole hotel

Padstow harbour

14

Rick Stein's Seafood
Restaurant, Riverside

The ferry to Rock

Padstow has been attracting visitors for a long time. More than 4,000 years ago, even before the building of the Pyramids, it's thought that travellers used the Fowey and Camel Valleys on their journeys from Brittany to Ireland. By using this route, known as 'The Saints Way', the tortuous sea passage around Land's End could be avoided.

The arrival of the railway in 1899 promoted Padstow to a major holiday destination. Until 1964, it was served by the Atlantic Coast Express – a direct train service from London – but the station closed in 1967. The old railway line is now the Camel Trail, a picturesque foot and cycle path along the river. One of the railway mileposts is now embedded outside the Shipwright's Arms public house on the Harbour Front

Padstow enjoys a mild and benign climate and a more sheltered position than other Cornish resorts. Sloping down to the harbour, where many fine medieval buildings survive, the town is a wonderful jumble of crooked streets and multifarious little shops, which have developed organically over the years without hindrance by the heavy hand of town planners.

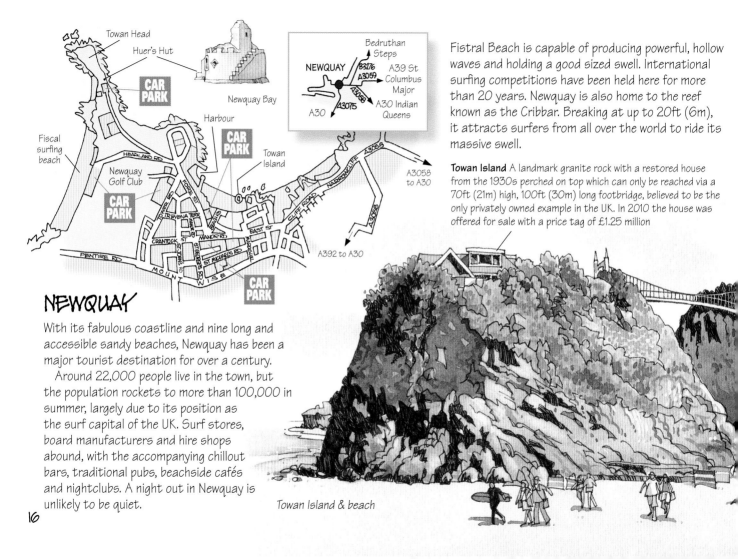

Towan Head

Huer's Hut

Newquay Bay

CAR PARK

Harbour

CAR PARK

Towan Island

Fiscal surfing beach

HEADLAND RD

Newquay Golf Club

CAR PARK

FORE ST

TO TREVENA TERR

MANOR RD

EAST ST

CLIFF ROAD

NARROWCLIFF

A3058

A3058 to A30

CRANTOCK ST

ST JOHNS RD

ST GEORGES RD

ST MICHAEL'S RD

MARCUS HILL

PENTIRE RD

MOUNT WISE

CAR PARK

A392 to A30

NEWQUAY
Bedruthan Steps
B3176
A3059
A39 St Columbus Major
A3058
A3075
A30 Indian Queens
A30

NEWQUAY

With its fabulous coastline and nine long and accessible sandy beaches, Newquay has been a major tourist destination for over a century.

Around 22,000 people live in the town, but the population rockets to more than 100,000 in summer, largely due to its position as the surf capital of the UK. Surf stores, board manufacturers and hire shops abound, with the accompanying chillout bars, traditional pubs, beachside cafés and nightclubs. A night out in Newquay is unlikely to be quiet.

Towan Island & beach

Fistral Beach is capable of producing powerful, hollow waves and holding a good sized swell. International surfing competitions have been held here for more than 20 years. Newquay is also home to the reef known as the Cribbar. Breaking at up to 20ft (6m), it attracts surfers from all over the world to ride its massive swell.

Towan Island A landmark granite rock with a restored house from the 1930s perched on top which can only be reached via a 70ft (21m) high, 100ft (30m) long footbridge, believed to be the only privately owned example in the UK. In 2010 the house was offered for sale with a price tag of £1.25 million

For a quieter time head for Towan Head, a breezy, open peninsula with good walks and sea views. An ancient stone hut on the Head once housed a huer who alerted the town's fishermen of approaching pilchard shoals with cries of 'Hevva, Hevva!' ('Here they are!'). With the harbour almost a mile away he must have been a remarkable shouter.

The Steps from the clifftop

BEDRUTHAN STEPS

Six miles northeast of Newquay the cliffs at Bedruthan have been systematically eroded, leaving a series of volcanic rock stacks which rise majestically from Bedruthan Beach, forming a spectacular series of columns stretching across the bay.

There's ample parking in a National Trust car park and a precipitous series of steps have been cut into the rock down to the beach. The descent should not be attempted lightly but it's hugely satisfying to walk amongst the towers and witness the power of the sea close up. The beach is beautiful white sand and it's easy to linger too long with the tide coming in and the steep climb back up the cliff to accomplish. Take care!

17

ST AGNES

A large, sprawling but attractive, village built on a hillside, St Agnes boasts a remarkable range of shops including grocers, butchers, greengrocers, a pharmacy, newsagent, post office, and even a bank! A stroll along Vicarage Road to the church is like stepping back in time. There are also craft shops, galleries and workshops.

St Agnes parish church consecrated in 1851 and built on the site of earlier buildings dating back to the early 1300s

Bank House Grade II listed built early 19th century

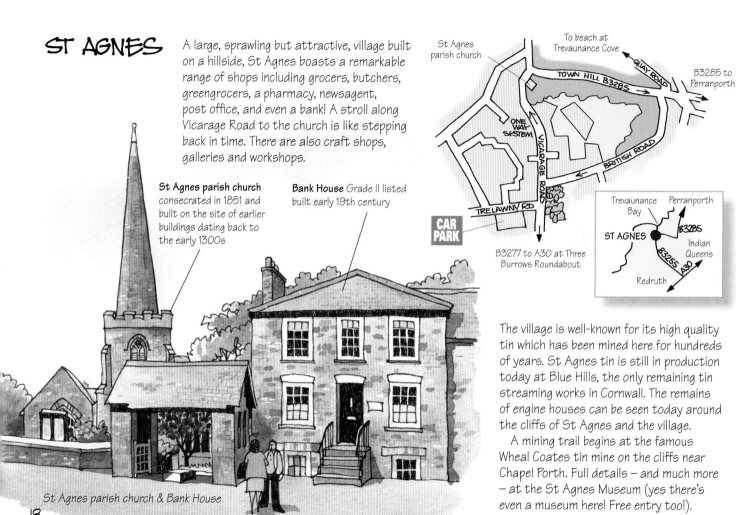

St Agnes parish church
To beach at Trevaunance Cove
QUAY ROAD
TOWN HILL B3285
B3285 to Perranporth
ONE WAY SYSTEM
VICARAGE ROAD
BRITISH ROAD
TRELAWNY RD
CAR PARK
B3277 to A30 at Three Burrows Roundabout

Trevaunance Bay
Perranporth
ST AGNES
B3285
Indian Queens
B3255
A30
Redruth

St Agnes parish church & Bank House

The village is well-known for its high quality tin which has been mined here for hundreds of years. St Agnes tin is still in production today at Blue Hills, the only remaining tin streaming works in Cornwall. The remains of engine houses can be seen today around the cliffs of St Agnes and the village.

A mining trail begins at the famous Wheal Coates tin mine on the cliffs near Chapel Porth. Full details – and much more – at the St Agnes Museum (yes there's even a museum here! Free entry too!).

18

Central shops

Trevaunance Bay is a half mile away from the village along a pleasant wooded minor road, Quay Road. There's a car park at the end and all the seaside facilites you'd expect.

The scene is impressive, nature in the raw. A restless sea rattles a stoney beach beneath cliffs pitted and crumbling from centuries of Atlantic storms and stained by mineral deposits. Heaps of mining waste are piled across the skyline while seagulls soar in endless flight.

There have been repeated attempts to build a harbour here. The Tonkin family was most successful in 1710, their pier surviving for over a century. A new one was built but that too was soon washed away. Trevaunance Bay remains pierless. Nature always wins.

Trevaunance Bay

PORTHTOWAN

St Agnes
PORTHTOWAN
Indian Queens
Porthreath
A30
Hayle
Redruth

The popular resort of Porthtowan lies along a narrow combe leading to a broad shore where golden sands and rolling Atlantic rollers are a delight for surfers. Now a virtual holiday complex, the village was once a hugely prosperous copper mining centre. Wheal Towan, which overlooked the village, was said to yield its owner, Ralph Allen Daniell of Trelissick, a fortune of 'a guinea a minute' night and day.

When the decline set in towards the end of the 19th century there was a mass exodus to mining camps in California, where miners from Porthtowan outnumbered the rest. They took their homespun standards with them – no work on Sundays, put on your best clothes and attend chapel.

Porthtowan hit the national headlines in February 2010 when a 56ft (17m) long Fin whale, thought to have been hit by a ship, was washed up on the beach.

Ruined engine house near Porthtowan

A ride between the brown, stoney hills inland from Porthtowan is a rather surreal experience after the green fields and golden sands along the coast. The valley once reverberated with all the clamour of the 19th-century mining industry, but is now silent and still.

With carefree scenes of modern holiday makers not far away, it's a good place to reflect on the hard lives that miners and their families endured in less fortunate times.

CAR PARK

Porthtowan from the Beach Road

20

PORTREATH

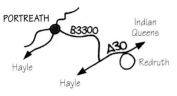

Like neighbouring Porthtowan, Porthreath is now a thriving holiday village. It was also once an industrial hot spot. But at Porthreath it was much, much more so!

In 1760, mining and industry magnet, Lord de Dunstanville, set out to transform the quiet little fishing village into a viable port with docks and a railway. A three foot (one metre) gauge tramway to Scorrier was in operation by 1812 and a branchline with a 1 in 7 incline down to the harbour was laid to join the Hayle railway. The harbour was expanded in 1800, 1824 and 1846. Copper was transported from mines in the Chacewater area using horse drawn wagons and shipped to Swansea for smelting, while coal and timber were brought in for use in the mines. Modern boats still find the narrow harbour entrance difficult to negotiate so it must have been really hairy with a large sailing ship carrying more than 100 tons of ore.

The railways and tramways associated with the mineral trade have now been turned into an excellent long distance cycleway and footpath, extending 15 miles from Portreath to Devoran on the south coast.

The inner harbour

Portreath from Tregea Hill

CAR PARK

The harbour

Godrevy Head is a rocky, one-mile square promontory, facing north into the Atlantic, largely owned and managed by the National Trust. It has some of the best coastal heathland in Cornwall, with many species of plant, animal and insect life, and is a renowned habitat for seabirds. Grey seals populate one of the coves. Godrevy is a wonderful place to walk, picnic and explore the rock formations and pools when the tide is out.

Godrevy Island lies approx three hundred yards off the Head. Seaward of Godrevy Island lies a submerged reef known as The Stones. Godrevy lighthouse was built to warn shipping of the dangerous reef.

GODREVY & HAYLE TOWANS

The beach and Godrevy lighthouse

Godrevy Lighthouse

The lighthouse was built on Godrevy Island in 1858–1859, a white octagonal tower, 86ft (26m) high, made of rubble-stone and mortar. Originally, the light was continuously manned by three men, but in 1934 it was automated. The light flashes white/red every 10 seconds and can be seen from around 12 miles away, with a red sector only being visible in the arc of danger from the reef.

Three miles of golden sands, cosy dunes that give respite against the fresh Atlantic winds and a view of a lighthouse with a famous literary connection. Little wonder then, that when Hayle Towans was put up for sale at auction a few years ago it sparked a fierce bidding war across the world. The plot, covering 76 acres, eventually sold for £80,000 to an unnamed woman with Cornish connections. She's not allowed to develop it, dig it up or stop other people using it. Her desire appears to be simply to own a little piece of paradise and keep it that way. How wonderful is that?

The beach, across the bay from St Ives, is a favourite among surfers, walkers and those who like to lounge on the sand or in the dunes. It also attracts attention from literary pilgrims. The lighthouse that sits so attractively on rocky Godrevy Island is widely believed to have been the inspiration for Virginia Woolf's 1927 novel, *To the Lighthouse*. As a child, Woolf and her family took holidays in St Ives.

The Towans

23

ST IVES

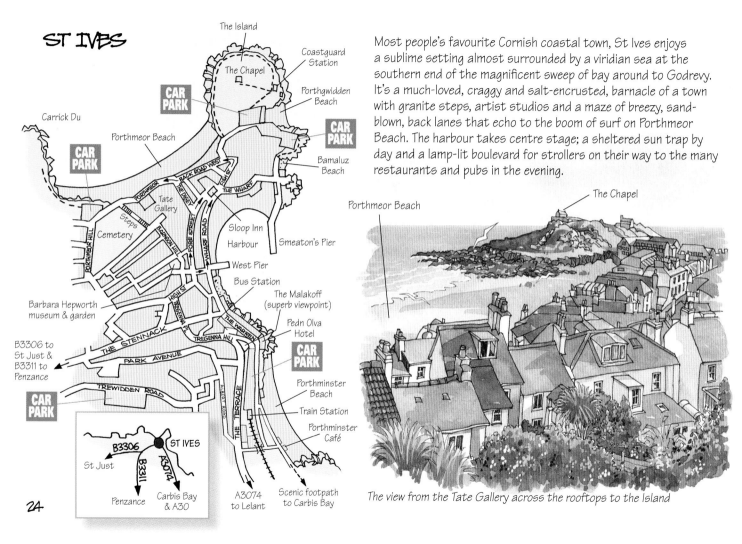

Most people's favourite Cornish coastal town, St Ives enjoys a sublime setting almost surrounded by a viridian sea at the southern end of the magnificent sweep of bay around to Godrevy. It's a much-loved, craggy and salt-encrusted, barnacle of a town with granite steps, artist studios and a maze of breezy, sand-blown, back lanes that echo to the boom of surf on Porthmeor Beach. The harbour takes centre stage; a sheltered sun trap by day and a lamp-lit boulevard for strollers on their way to the many restaurants and pubs in the evening.

The Island

The Chapel

Coastguard Station

Porthgwidden Beach

CAR PARK

CAR PARK

Carrick Du

Porthmeor Beach

Bamaluz Beach

CAR PARK

PORTHMEOR

BACK ROAD WEST

FISH ST

THE DIGEY

THE WHARF

Tate Gallery

Steps

WHARF ROAD

FORE STREET

Cemetery

PORTHMEOR HILL

BARNOON HILL

Sloop Inn

Harbour

West Pier

Smeaton's Pier

Bus Station

HIGH ST

TREGENNA PL

The Malakoff (superb viewpoint)

Barbara Hepworth museum & garden

Pedn Olva Hotel

THE STENNACK

THE WARREN

TREGENNA HILL

B3306 to St Just & B3311 to Penzance

PARK AVENUE

CAR PARK

Porthminster Beach

TREWIDDEN ROAD

ALBERT ROAD

CAR PARK

Train Station

Porthminster Café

THE TERRACE

B3306

ST IVES

St Just

B3311

A3074

Penzance

Carbis Bay & A30

A3074 to Lelant

Scenic footpath to Carbis Bay

Porthmeor Beach

The Chapel

The view from the Tate Gallery across the rooftops to the Island

24

During the 1800s, St Ives was a hugely prosperous fishing town. The pilchard (sardine) industry was especially profitable with around 300 seine boats netting millions of fish. At one time 800 men and boys were employed with 400 boats.

In 1834 there was possibly the largest catch ever, when 30 million pilchards were caught in one net in one hour. The pilchards were salted and pressed into barrels along the seashore and exported mainly to Italy, where they were the preferred dish to eat on Fridays.

The arrival of the railway in 1877 began the change from an industrial town to a tourist destination. GWR was known as 'God's Wonderful Railway'.

Attracted by the bohemian lifestyle – and the bright light – avant-garde artists flocked to St Ives and each year hired a whole train carriage to take their paintings to be exhibited in London. For a few dazzling years the remote little town was as artistically famous as Paris or New York.

Bolstered by the arrival of Tate St Ives, the contemporary art scene continues to flourish, but the local fishing industry is greatly diminished. Recently, single line fishing for mackerel has become popular, and more cost effective, as it's conducted by a lone fisherman in a small boat.

Coastwatch station Originally an abandoned Coastguard station but reopened in 1994 by the National Coastwatch Institution (NCI), a charity manned by volunteers

The Island

Smeaton's Pier built in 1770, designed by John Smeaton who was also responsible for the Eddystone Lighthouse

The classic view of St Ives from The Malakoff

25

A walk around the Island is highly recommended, and is especially exciting when there's a stormy sea and the power of the breaking waves shake the ground under your feet.

The granite-built Chapel of St Nicholas, standing proudly atop the island, has been a seaman's chapel, customs' lookout and part of the war office. Threatened with demolition in 1904, it was saved by fierce local opposition. The simple medieval chapel is now a cherished symbol of old St Ives, where occasional services are held.

Tate St Ives was opened in 1993 by Prince Charles (no lover of contemporary art), replacing an old gas works eyesore. Whatever you may think of modern art (and we all have an opinion), it's generally agreed that the building overlooking the Porthmeor surfing beach is mightily impressive.

Tate St Ives & Porthmeor Beach from the Island

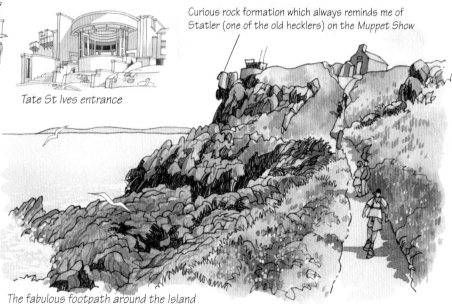

Curious rock formation which always reminds me of Statler (one of the old hecklers) on the Muppet Show

Tate St Ives entrance

The Chapel of St Nicholas

The fabulous footpath around the Island

Tregenna Hill

Lighthouse 1890, Smeaton's Pier

Lighthouse 1831, Smeaton's Pier

The problems of parking in St Ives are legendary. Space has simply run out. Canny local residents with empty drives to their homes make easy money renting them out as visitors' parking places.

If you're staying for a holiday make sure there's private car parking included in your booking. For a day visit you need to park early. By far the best option for day trippers, is to park at Lelant and take the train to St Ives – one of the most scenic rail routes in Britain.

There are plans to extend the Tate, the old artist's painting lofts are being tarted up and 'cultural tourism' is the new buzz word, but I still love St Ives for it's ramshackle beauty and raffish independence. There's nowhere quite like St Ives.

Sloop Inn

27

THE B3306 ST IVES TO ST JUST ROAD

Porthmeor Farm, Higher Porthmeor

Not so much a road, more an ancient track, twisting and squirming across a landscape that's hardly changed since the Iron Age. On one side loom the moors of west Penwin, a pagan world of standing stones and bracken-covered hillsides, punctured by dramatic granite outcrops. The other side of the road is a mosaic of crooked fields and thrown-together stone walls. In places the road runs below the level of the fields and you're in a rock cutting where wild flowers sprout profusely. Trees are stunted and bizarrely twisted towards the hills. As you travel west there's the constant feeling that the land is running out, and the ocean twinkling away on your right is preparing to take over.

This is a route to savour and shouldn't be rushed. Pick your time, evening is a good bet but inevitably it can became extremely busy in summer. Be patient, this is a precious place.

Along the road there's one of the greatest concentrations of mines in Cornwall. The Carn Galver Mine and engine house ruins near Rosemergy has a small car park and is a good place to stop. The engine house with the chimney once housed a 40in (100cm) pumping engine and a smaller building to the east had a 20in (50cm) cylinder.

Carn Galver Mine ruins

Porthmoina Cove   Bosigran Cliff

Rosemergy

Rosemergy is a picturesque collection of farm buildings and holiday cottages between Morvah and Higher Porthmeor. There's an excellent tea garden open during the day in summer, with parking. Down the road towards St Just, a footpath goes across fields to join the coastal footpath near Porthmoina Cove.

Morvah is a small village straddling the B3306. It's mainly housing plus a farm and St Bridget's parish church. There's record of a settlement here in the early Middle Ages. In 1884, a hoard of gold bracelets were discovered at nearby Carne Farm, thought to be payment in a tin trading deal .

Morvah

Zennor lies just off the B3306, a compact little village set in a dip, always a pleasure to behold with its perfect composition of country road sweeping past the pub to the church. It was once a centre for fishing, quarrying, farming and tin mining, but now only agriculture survives.

The *Tinner's Arms* is noted for its former famous residents, the novelist D.H. Lawrence and his German wife Frieda, who lodged there in 1916 before renting a cottage nearby. Lawrence wrote *Women in Love* during their 18-month stay, before they were ousted for their bohemian lifestyle. Members of the community also thought that the strangers were spies.

Church of St Senara Parts of the building date to the 13th century, but it's most famous for a carving of a mermaid on the end of a bench said to be more than 600 years old. Legend has it that a mermaid lured the squire's son to her home in the watery depths. He was never seen again but his beautiful singing voice can still be heard

ZENNOR

Wayside Museum a collection of more than 5,000 local relics built up over 60 years

The Tinners' Arms Built in 1271 to accommodate the masons building the church

Youth hostel in an old congregational chapel

Zennor

PENDEEN WATCH

Guardian of the rocky outcrop of Pendeen New Cliff and The Wra rocks offshore, Pendeen Watch (or lighthouse) is accessed down a minor road north of the village of Pendeen.

The 60ft (17m) high tower was commissioned in 1900 with a paraffin-fuelled, five-wick Argand lamp, which was replaced in 1926 by an electric one. The lighthouse was automated in 1995 and the keepers left. The cottages where they and their families lived have been updated and are now holiday lets. The light can be seen from 16 miles away and the mournful blast of the fog horn sounds once every 20 seconds, but fortunately for visitors in the cottages, only when it's foggy.

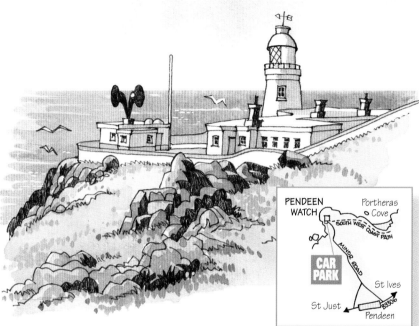

This is a good place to join the South West Coast Path. A wonderful stroll of about a mile east brings you to Portheras Cove, a 'secret' and unspoilt hideaway with a fabulous beach.

Walk southwest along the route and you're soon into mining country, where a series of evocative old buildings lines the coast. There's evidence of mining activity in this area for over 3,000 years.

Geever tin mine operated between 1911 and 1990, during which it produced around 50,000 tons of black tin. The 67-acre site, the largest preserved mine site in the country, is now an award-winning museum and heritage centre.

Portheras Cove

31

ST JUST

In the 19th century, St Just-in-Penwith (to distinguish it from St Just-in-Roseland – a very different place!) was the centre of the tin and copper mining industry in this part of Cornwall.

The 20th century brought decline and a plan to make St Just the terminus of the main rail link to London was abandoned. The town was remote and forgotten.

However there are now signs of a revival in St Just's fortunes and there's plenty here to interest the discerning visitor.

St Just Square

The scars of hard times are evident around some of the granite streets of St Just, but the cheery centre is a good place to park and explore. There's a fine 14th-century pub, the King's Arms, an ancient church established in AD 596, and plenty of interesting galleries.

St Just is the most westerly town in mainland Britain and the smallest town in Cornwall. Another little-known claim to fame is that it's the English town that's furthest away from a motorway.

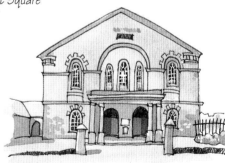

Methodist Chapel at the end of Chapel Street

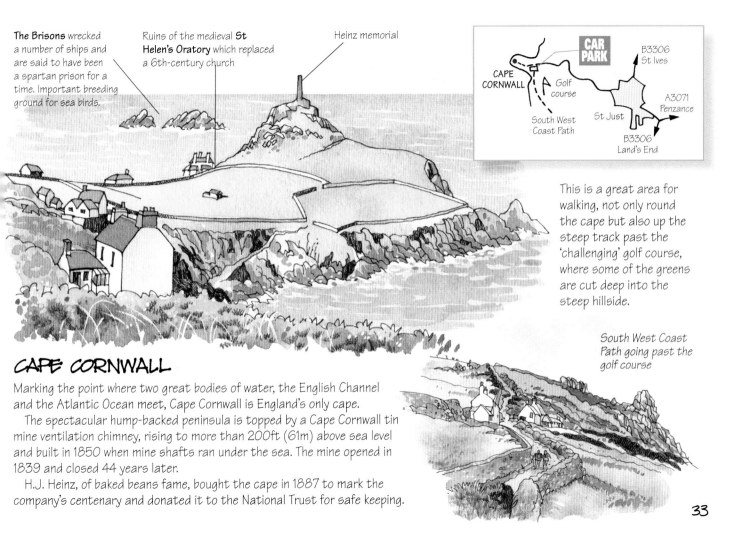

The Brisons wrecked a number of ships and are said to have been a spartan prison for a time. Important breeding ground for sea birds.

Ruins of the medieval St Helen's Oratory which replaced a 6th-century church

Heinz memorial

CAR PARK

CAPE CORNWALL

B3306 St Ives

Golf course

A3071 Penzance

South West Coast Path

St Just

B3306 Land's End

This is a great area for walking, not only round the cape but also up the steep track past the 'challenging' golf course, where some of the greens are cut deep into the steep hillside.

South West Coast Path going past the golf course

CAPE CORNWALL

Marking the point where two great bodies of water, the English Channel and the Atlantic Ocean meet, Cape Cornwall is England's only cape.

The spectacular hump-backed peninsula is topped by a Cape Cornwall tin mine ventilation chimney, rising to more than 200ft (61m) above sea level and built in 1850 when mine shafts ran under the sea. The mine opened in 1839 and closed 44 years later.

H.J. Heinz, of baked beans fame, bought the cape in 1887 to mark the company's centenary and donated it to the National Trust for safe keeping.

33

SENNEN COVE

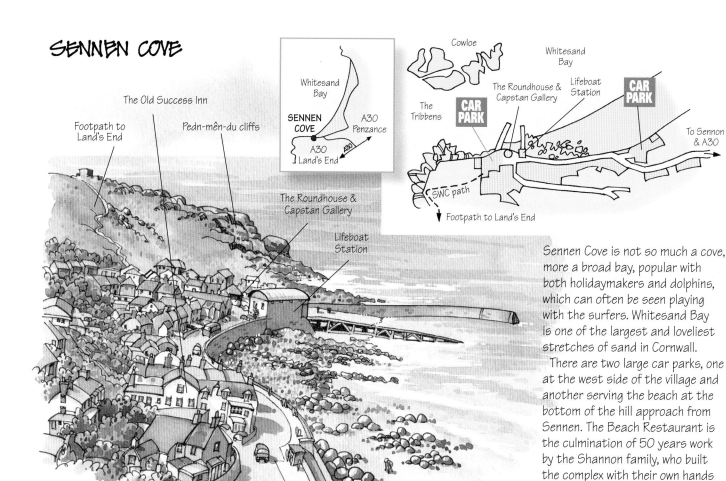

Inset map labels:

Whitesand Bay

SENNEN COVE

A30 Penzance

A30 Land's End

Upper right map labels:

Cowloe

Whitesand Bay

The Tribbens

CAR PARK

The Roundhouse & Capstan Gallery

Lifeboat Station

CAR PARK

To Sennon & A30

SWC path

Footpath to Land's End

Illustration labels:

The Old Success Inn

Footpath to Land's End

Pedn-mên-du cliffs

The Roundhouse & Capstan Gallery

Lifeboat Station

Sennen Cove is not so much a cove, more a broad bay, popular with both holidaymakers and dolphins, which can often be seen playing with the surfers. Whitesand Bay is one of the largest and loveliest stretches of sand in Cornwall.

There are two large car parks, one at the west side of the village and another serving the beach at the bottom of the hill approach from Sennen. The Beach Restaurant is the culmination of 50 years work by the Shannon family, who built the complex with their own hands beginning with a small beach café in 1959 and completed in 2004.

Cape Cornwall

Fishing boats on the beach

The lifeboat station was founded in 1853 and is manned by crew of 24 on call 24 hours a day. The station is unique in having two slipways, allowing the lifeboat to be recovered in the shelter of the breakwater at high tide or up the launching slipway at low tide.

The picturesque Roundhouse & Capstan Gallery, now an art gallery and gift shop, was originally used to winch boats up the beach. Protected by a long breakwater built in 1908, a small fishing fleet survives, its boats and paraphernalia littering a small beach.

A visit to Sennen Cove is always worthwhile, but for the total experience try going during a storm, when the waves are spectacular and spray crashes over the top of the Pedn-mên-du cliffs. Awesome.

The village lies at the western end of the bay and its grey-stone houses and white-painted hotels have over the years gradually crept up the hillside. The oddly-named Old Success Inn, a 17th-century former fisherman's inn, is prominent along the roadside.

Listen out for the 'Sennen Whooper' a strange whooping sound that legend says is heard through a mist, and is able to predict storms and prevent fishermen from setting sail.

The Roundhouse & Capstan Gallery

The village from the beach

35

LAND'S END WALK

Look out for the wreck of RMS Mulheim in narrow Gramper Bay. The ship ran aground in 2003 and its cargo of plastic scrap was safely removed. There was no loss of life or injury to the crew and the ship was left to break up 'naturally'. That's taking time to accomplish, but in the meantime the wreck has become a tourist attraction.

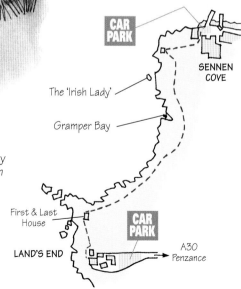

Sennen Cove & Whitesand Bay from the Land's End footpath

The mile or so walk along the clifftops is by far the best way to approach Land's End. There's a steep climb from the car park at Sennen Cove but that's easily compensated for with a fantastic view across the thatched rooftops of the village to Whitesand Bay. After reaching the lookout at the top of Pedn-mên-du, the route is obvious – just follow the crowds!

Longships Lighthouse tower originally built in 1795 with a replacement lit in 1873. Unmanned since 1988. The light has a range of 11 miles and flashes every ten seconds.

First & Last House, Land's End

In 1987 Peter de Savary purchased Land's End for almost £7 million. He built two new buildings and much of the present theme park. The current owners acquired it in 1996. The 'attractions' of the theme park depend on your taste, but the terrace of the Land's End Hotel is still a good place to enjoy a drink and the view of the spectacular granite cliffs. On a clear day, the Isles of Scilly can be seen on the horizon, and about six miles southwest, the Wolf Rock Lighthouse.

The story of the **'Irish Lady'** is one of Cornwall's romantic legends. During a storm an Irish ship was wrecked on this rock. The crew all perished but for two days and nights a woman passenger was seen sitting on the rock. Rescue was impossible due to the mountainous seas. When the storm finally ceased, the woman had gone but fishermen swear they still see her sitting weeping on the rock whenever a storm is threatened.

The 'Irish Lady' rock formation

Plenty of fine sea views

Land's End

37

PORTHCURNO

The Logan Rock is a rocking stone balanced apparently precariously on top of the saw-tooth promontory east of Porthcurno. Although it weighs some 80 tons, it was dislodged in 1824 by a group of over-refreshed British sailors. Following complaints from local residents for whom the rock had become a tourist attraction and source of income, the seamen were forced to restore it to its previous position. Today the Logan Rock still rocks, but not as easily as it did in the past.

Logan Rock

Porthcurno Beach

The bay has been voted one of the most beautiful in Europe and the beach is so perfect that you feel as though you can only walk on it in bare feet. Porthcurno has a lot going for it.

The village is also internationally-famous as the British termination of early submarine telegraph cables, the first of which was landed in 1870, part of a link stretching from the UK to India. A telecommunications college opened in 1950. After it closed in 1993, the Porthcurno Telegraph Museum was established, which includes tunnels cut into the hillsides for security during the war as part of the exhibits.

Porthcurno Telegraph Museum

The village and car park

MINACK THEATRE

A footpath cut into the cliffside from Porthcurno Beach climbs steeply to the astounding Minack Theatre, an open-air auditorium constructed in classical Greek style by the remarkable Rowena Cade. She was born in Derbyshire where her father owned a cotton mill. After his death, mother and daughter rented a house in Lamorna and when Rowena discovered the nearby Minack headland she bought it for £100. She built them a house there – with her own hands. Then came the idea for a theatre. With the help of two local men, Billy Rawlings and Tom Angove, she worked tirelessly on the theatre from 1931 until her death, aged 89, in 1983.

The airy footpath to the Minack theatre from Porthcurno Beach

The theatre

Unable to afford the cost of using granite throughout the theatre, Rowena developed her own technique for working with cement. Using the tip of an old screwdriver she decorated the backs of the seats with lettering and intricate Celtic designs before they hardened.

The theatre has its own car park and is open (along with its exotic garden) on most days of the year. From May to September drama, musicals and opera are performed in this most dramatic and unusual of settings.

Visitors cars aren't allowed access to Penberth Cove. There's limited parking for a few vehicles at the end of the road, leaving a walk of around 200 yards to the beach. The cove has no public facilities.

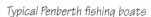
Typical Penberth fishing boats

PENBERTH COVE

A handful of cottages set in a peaceful valley running down to the sea. A tiny working harbour with a granite cobbled slipway and a tumbling stream crossed by a clapper-style bridge. There's not a lot at Penberth. But what there is adds up to a remarkably tranquil and picturesque scene which probably hasn't changed much for a hundred years. Only the granite rock, worn rounded and smooth by the wind and sea, bears witness to the passing of time.

The Cove still supports a few fishing boats which are now hauled up the slip (or cauance as it's known locally) by an electric winch, rather than the spectacular capstan. Mackerel, lobster and crab are the main catch, though their numbers have declined sharply since the 1980s.

The Cove

LAMORNA COVE

The granite quarries around here haven't been worked for 90 years, but their product is evident in the massive walls of the harbour. Lamorna Cove lies at the head of an attractive wooded valley where daffodils abound in the spring. Flowers were once grown commercially in the small fields. Granite from Lamorna Cove has been widely used in construction, most notably in the Thames Embankment and the nearby church of St Buryan, whose 92ft (28m) high granite tower is an imposing local landmark often used as a sight line by fishermen entering port.

The cafe and car park

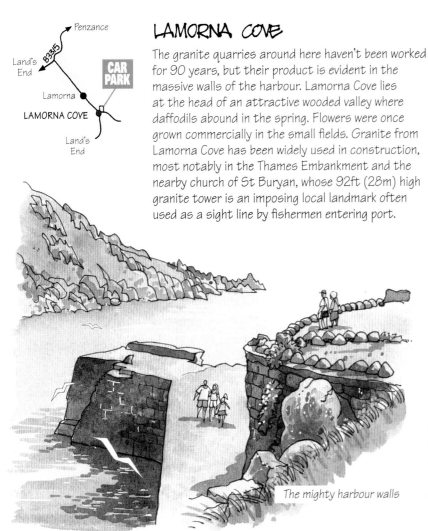

The mighty harbour walls

The cove has an excellent beach café with an elevated terrace, a fine place to unwind and maybe watch divers setting out to explore Bucks Reef or one of the many shipwrecks lying offshore.

It's remarkable how many of these little coves there are around the far West – and they're all different.

41

A hugely popular tourist magnet, but even the most cynical visitor admits 'there's something about Mousehole'. With miniscule, winding streets (a nightmare to drive through), cramped fishermans' cottages, interesting galleries, a pretty harbour fringed by golden sand (imported) and an open aspect to Mount's Bay, there definitely is something about Mousehole (always pronounced 'Mowzel').

Along with Marazion, the village was until the 16th century, one of the most important ports on Mount's Bay. In 1595, Mousehole was destroyed along with Penzance, Newlyn and Paul in a devastating attack by Spanish raiders. The only surviving building in the village was the Keigwin Arms, a local inn. Now a private residence, the building bears a plaque which says 'Squire Jenkyn Keigwin was killed here, 23rd July 1595, defending this house against the Spaniards'.

Ancient harbourside buildings along the beach

42

The classic view across the harbour

MOUSEHOLE

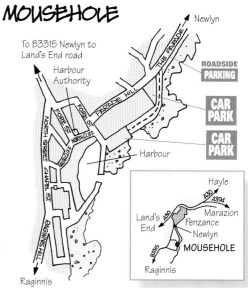

The Harbour Authority building

Like most of the desirable coastal villages in Cornwall, Mousehole has seen an increase in second home ownership and a corresponding decline in resident population. Even the village's historic harbourside hotel, the Lobster Pot, has been turned into modern luxury apartments. In the 1930s it was a guest house run by Wyn Henderson, friend to the Welsh poet Dylan Thomas, who spent his honeymoon here after marrying Caitlin Macnamara at Penzance register office.

Mousehole is still a great place to visit, although parking can be a problem. Get there early or go out of season.

The village of Mousehole developed around its harbour and the fishing fleet that sustained it, appearing in the record books as an important fishing port from as early as 1266. Part of the south quay originates from 1390, possibly the oldest pier in Cornwall.

The fishing industry has declined drastically over the last 100 years, but a handful of boats maintain the long heritage and tradition of a working harbour, while the majority of vessels now lying at anchor are pleasure craft.

During the winter months, sturdy wooden beams are used to close the harbour entrance, keeping the force of the sea at bay and protecting the village.

The north side of the substantial harbour wall

A quayside doorway

Just before Christmas 1981, news from Mousehole shocked the nation. During an attempted rescue in hurricane-force winds of people on the stricken *Union Star* off Porthcurno, the Mousehole lifeboat, the *Solomon Brown*, and its entire crew of eight were lost. The eight crew and passengers on the ship also died.

In 1983, the lifeboat was moved to Newlyn but continues to be known as the 'Penlee Lifeboat'. The old station remains on the edge of Mousehole, left just as it was on that terrible night as a poignant memorial to those who died.

Mousehole Christmas lights are famous throughout Cornwall. There are even helicopter trips from Penzance to see them from the sky. But on the 19th of December each year they are turned off for an hour to remember those who were lost.

The 'Mousehole' gift shop

The former Keigwin Arms

From the harbour wall –
a great place for nosey looks into fishing boats

Another quayside doorway

NEWLYN

Though joined to Penzance, Newlyn retains its own strong identity. It's home to the largest fishing fleet in the UK with more than 600 registered boats and some 40 acres of harbour. Still ungentrified by incomers, it also looks and feels like a working port. You don't come to Newlyn for the shopping – unless it's for fish.

Newlyn was rebuilt after the Spanish raid in the 16th century but little of the old town remains. Many of the white-painted or stone-faced cottages separated by narrow alleys were only saved from demolition by the outbreak of the Second World War.

Walk up any of the roads leading steeply uphill from the harbour for some great views across the bay to St Michael's Mount.

Trewarveneth Road

Typical Newlyn fishing boat

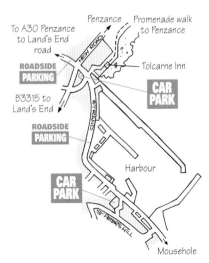

Iconic harbourside buildings from the Strand

A statue of Sir Humphry Davy, born in Penzance during 1778, occupies a prominent position in front of the Market House, despite him leaving the town as a child. Davy invented the safety lamp in 1815, which reduced the risk of underground explosions and saved many miners' lives, including local ones.

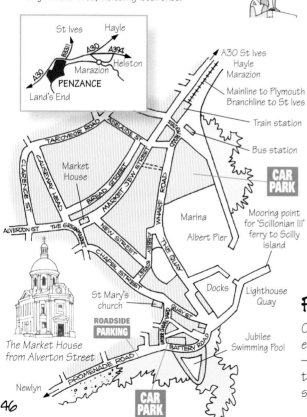

The Market House from Alverton Street

ROADSIDE PARKING

CAR PARK

St Ives
Hayle
Marazion
PENZANCE
Land's End
Helston

Market House

A30 St Ives
Hayle
Marazion

Mainline to Plymouth
Branchline to St Ives

Train station

Bus station

CAR PARK

Marina

Albert Pier

Mooring point for 'Scillonian III' ferry to Scilly island

St Mary's church

Docks

Lighthouse Quay

Jubilee Swimming Pool

Newlyn

TAROVEOR ROAD
ADELAIDE ST
CAUSEWAY HEAD
CLARENCE ST
ALVERTON ST
THE GREENMARKET
BREAD STREET
MARKET JEW STREET
NEW STREET
CHAPEL STREET
JENNINGS ST
WHARF ROAD
STATION ROAD
THE QUAY
QUAY ST
UNION DARKS YARD
BATTERY ROAD
PROMENADE ROAD

Market House

Sir Humphry Davy Statue

Market Jew Street

PENZANCE

Once a fashionable seaside resort, Penzance is now a little frayed around the edges, but is still a popular tourist destination with an attractive promenade – the only one in Cornwall – and some elegant Georgian architecture. The town's harbour is the most westerly on the English Channel, from where ferry services operate to the Isles of Scilly, some 28 miles beyond Land's End.

Difficult to believe these days, but Marazion and Mousehole were once more important ports than Penzance. However, in the 18th century the town caught up, becoming a leading light in the tin trade. The quay was rebuilt and lengthened in 1782. Albert Pier opened in 1847 and lines were laid for trains to reach the harbourside in 1852. The inner harbour, the 'floating dock', was finished in 1884.

Penzance harbour is still busy, building and maintaining ships and boats, and it's a fascinating place to wander round with all kinds of crafts to be seen.

Penzance is set on a hill with a mild climate and winter temperatures similar to those of Nice. Banana trees grow in domestic gardens and the quality of the light has attracted artists since the 19th century.

Visit the main shopping areas of Market Jew Street and the Causeway Head, then head down Chapel Street for a stroll along the prom' to the Tolcarne Inn at Newlyn for fresh crab sandwiches. On the way back there's some fine Georgian and Regency architecture to admire in the streets leading off the promenade.

There's a lot more to Penzance than you might think.

St Mary's church built between 1832 and 1835. Has ornate carvings, a stained-glass window over the altar and a balcony

Abbey Hotel Owned by icon of 'Swinging London' in the 1960s, Jean Shrimpton, and her husband. Now managed by their son Thaddeus and his family

Road from the station opened in 1866

Lighthouse built in 1855 on Lighthouse Quay

A fine panorama from the marina

47

Chapel Street, the town's original high street, is Penzance's most interesting and historic street. The Egyptian House, built in 1835 by a local eccentric mineralogist to house his collection of rocks, is a flamboyant extravaganza of striped columns, elaborate windows and weird cornices. Sitting uneasily amongst the architectural chaos, is the royal coat of arms. The facade fell into repair during the 1960s but was sensitively restored in 1973.

Opposite is the Union Hotel, which used to be the town's assembly rooms where the death of Nelson and the victory at Trafalgar were first announced on the mainland. A Penzance trawler had intercepted the warship carrying the news to Falmouth and the Mayor of Penzance made the announcement in what is now predictably called Nelson's Bar.

The Smuggler on the roof!

Chapel Street

Further down the street, the 17th-century Admiral Benbow pub is packed with maritime artifacts and memorabilia. It also has an armed smuggler on the roof. Nobody seems to know why but in this street it's not thought to be at all unusual!

The Chocolate House was built as a fisherman's cottage in the early 1700s. It eventually became a modern post office and when it closed, was converted to a shop selling hand-made chocolates. After a major refurbishment in 2008, the landmark building with its rococo-style ornate fascia of candy-striped columns and nude nymphs became a unique holiday home.

The Chocolate House

The Egyptian House

The Turk's Head is believed to be the oldest inn in the town, dating to the 13th century. A tunnel to the harbour was once used to transfer smuggled goods.

Further down the street, a plaque on a distinctive red-brick house marks the home of Maria Branwell, mother of the Bronte sisters.

The Dolphin Inn near the harbour is said to be the first place in Britain where tobacco was smoked and to have housed Sir John Hawkins, one of the three commanders of the English fleet during the wars with Spain. It was also the venue for the notorious trials presided over by Hanging Judge Jeffreys in the 17th century. Anything seems possible here.

The Turks Head

Captain Cutter's House is a long-established tobacconist with a huge range of tobaccos, pipes and cigars. With smoking now well-established as a disreputable habit the products are hidden away behind a flamboyant doorway perfectly suited to this remarkable street.

The Dolphin Inn, Battery Road

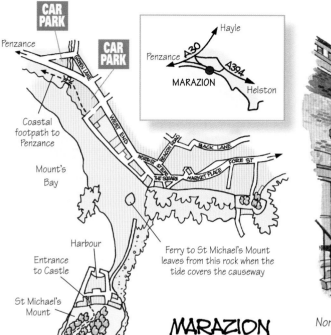

CAR PARK

CAR PARK

Penzance

GREEN LANE

Coastal footpath to Penzance

Mount's Bay

WEST END

NORTH ST

BACK LANE

THE SQUARE

MARKET PLACE

FORE ST

Harbour

Entrance to Castle

St Michael's Mount

The castle

Ferry to St Michael's Mount leaves from this rock when the tide covers the causeway

Hayle

Penzance A30

A394

MARAZION

Helston

North Street

MARAZION

Marazion was recorded in the Domesday Book of 1088 and is the oldest chartered town in Britain, having been granted this status by King Henry III in 1257. It's a long, narrow village strung along the eastern side of Mount's Bay with a twisting main street, frequently grid-locked by visitors in summer. They come to enjoy the safe, sandy beaches, windsurfing and kitesurfing. They travel many miles to witness the spectacular twice a year sight of thousands of starlings arriving at dusk to roost at the RSPB Reserve at Marazion Marsh. But most of all, people flock here from all over the world to visit the area's star attraction and national treasure, St Michael's Mount (see page 52).

The village itself is pleasant enough with attractive sun-drenched squares edged by galleries and various kinds of eateries. There are also some handsome houses to enjoy, a legacy of when Marazion prospered in the tin and copper trade. But inevitably it's glorious Mount's Bay, widely recognised as one of the most beautiful bays in the UK, that keeps grabbing the attention.

B&Bs off The Square

The Town Hall looks like something out of Toytown and has served many uses, from the town jail to the fire station. Formerly, it was St Thomas' Hall and later a Barclay's Bank. The much-loved landmark, built in 1871 in a French chateau style, is now a museum. A typical cell of the period has been built inside.

Another house in the square was where Charles II hid after his defeat at Naseby.

The streets climbing up the hill behind the village are worth exploring. The view back to St Michael's Mount and the bay will make you want to stay in Cornwall for ever.

It's possible to approach Marazion from the east side, but the drive through the crowded village isn't recommended. All the car parking is at the west end. It's usually adaquate but you never know how many people are going to turn up. In the summer – loads!

Camper vans usually line the straight roadside from the railway bridge, but if you can get in there the beach runs alongside. From here there's a hard-surfaced footpath going round the bay to Penzance.

The Town Hall

Seagrove Gallery Excellent paintings plus a boutique and tea garden

The Town Hall

The King's Arms

Out of the Blue Gallery owned by popular Cornish artist, Glyn Macey and his wife. Highly recommended

The Square

51

ST MICHAEL'S MOUNT

It's the stuff of fairytale and legend. An iconic castle on a slate and granite island rising to almost 230ft (70m) above sea level and dominating the bay. St Michael's Mount never disappoints.

The island's early life was more prosaic, the unromantic port for the fishermen of Marazion. After a vision of St Michael appeared in the 5th century a church was built, and by the 8th century a monastery had been founded. During the Civil War it was used as a Royalist stronghold, before becoming the home of the St Aubyn family in 1660, which continues to this day.

Set 400yds (365m) offshore, access to the Mount is a stimulating walk along a cobbled causeway or by ferry when it's covered by the tide.

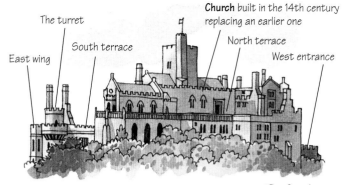

The turret

Church built in the 14th century replacing an earlier one

East wing

South terrace

North terrace

West entrance

The Castle

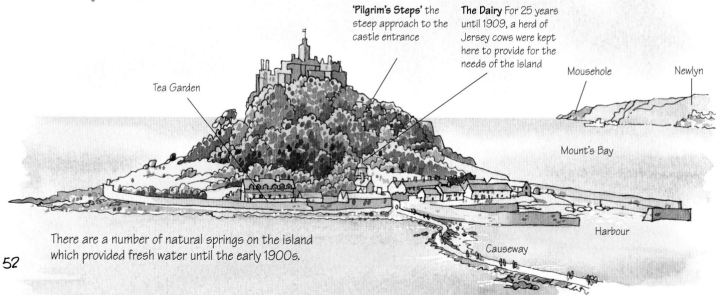

'Pilgrim's Steps' the steep approach to the castle entrance

The Dairy For 25 years until 1909, a herd of Jersey cows were kept here to provide for the needs of the island

Tea Garden

Mousehole

Newlyn

Mount's Bay

Harbour

Causeway

There are a number of natural springs on the island which provided fresh water until the early 1900s.

Most of the Mount was given to the National Trust in 1954. From the entrance a steep, tree-lined avenue climbs to the castle. Additions and modifications in a variety of architectural styles during the 17th to 19th centuries have added to its attractive Gothic appearance.

Inside it's remarkably cosy – for a castle – with paintings, family mementos and military items on display in the fine rooms. The views from the battlements are, of course, superlative.

No visitor to Cornwall should ever leave without a visit to St Michael's Mount. A walk across the causeway and a look round the harbour won't cost you a penny, except of course for some sustenance in the tea garden overlooking the sea.

Entrance to the castle & National Trust shop

From the harbour wall

The Mount end of the causeway

As we strolled along Marazion beach one barmy day a 'boat' approached from the Mount direction, heading at speed towards us.

'Wouldn't it be funny if it drove straight onto the beach?', I said to my wife, then watched open-mouthed as the 'boat' did just that.

It was our first sight of the Mount's amphibious service vehicle, and a wonderful surprise. Look out for it.

The Mount's amphibious vehicle

The prevailing south-west winds whip straight into Porthleven and the massive sea wall bears testament to the destructive power of the sea. In contrast to the more cutesy Cornish fishing villages, this is a no-nonsense kind of a place with a huge harbour built in the early 1800s to protect a fishing fleet of around 100 boats, and to provide safe landing for coal and timber supplies for the mines. A boat-building industry also developed and until the 1970s all manner of craft were launched from the slipway at the north end of the harbour.

Though much reduced from the time when a day's pilchards catch filled 2,000 barrels of 54-gallon capacity, fishing continues for mainly crab, lobster and crayfish.

The old industrial premises have been turned into a pleasant miscellany of craft galleries, restaurants or shops, and an assortment of terraces and fishermans' cottages overlook the harbour. Children climb on cannons recovered from the 19th century man o' war, HMS Anson, which sank nearby, while parents laze on the immense harbour walls or chatter outside the two salty pubs. All is tranquil.

That's on a day of clear skies and sunshine. When there's a gale brewing, look out!

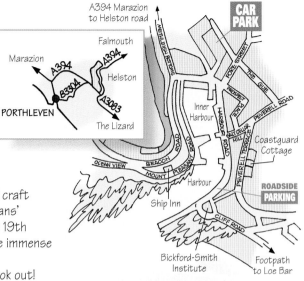

PORTHLEVEN

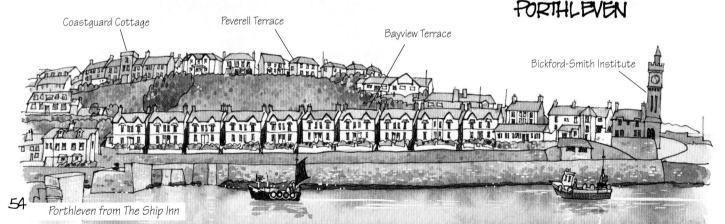

54 *Porthleven from The Ship Inn*

Bickford-Smith Institute

The east side harbour wall follows the beautiful curve of Bayview Terrace, a line of imposing white-painted villas, to the much-battered and worn stone pier. Here master surfers test their skills on waves surging along the pier wall and breaking on an alarming platform of sharp rocks. Not for the faint-hearted.

Nor is the pier area when a gale is at it's height, as you're likely to be blown over. Watched from a safe distance, the waves crashing over the sea wall is a spectacle that people travel many miles to see.

Steps behind the Institute climb up to Peverell Terrace, from where there's a fine view over the harbour. From Mount Pleasant Road there's a similar view from the west.

Cottage on Cliff Road

The Bickford-Smith Institute Porthleven's most recognisable icon. Built by Cornish fuse-maker and Liberal-Unionist MP William Bickford-Smith in 1882 as a scientific and literary centre. With a clocktower 70ft (20m) high, it looks like a church but isn't and never has been. Currently unused but has been a snooker club and once housed the town council offices. It featured as the incident room in the late 90s TV detective series, *Wycliffe*

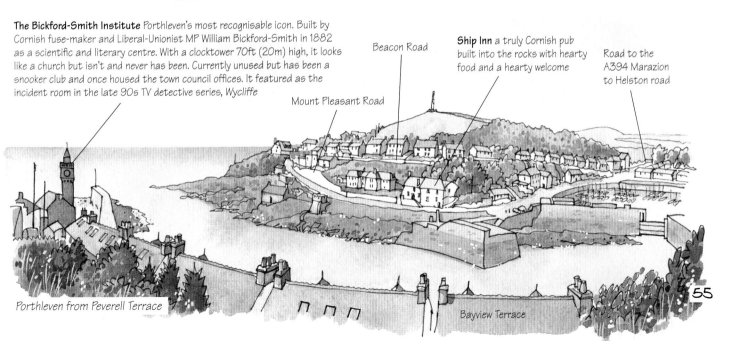

Beacon Road

Mount Pleasant Road

Ship Inn a truly Cornish pub built into the rocks with hearty food and a hearty welcome

Road to the A394 Marazion to Helston road

Porthleven from Peverell Terrace

Bayview Terrace

55

LOE BAR WALK

A remarkable natural feature, Loe Bar is a bank of smooth stones which cuts off the Cober Valley from the sea. The 200yds (183m) wide bar slopes steeply down to the sea and is thought to have been created by storms during the 12th century. Before then merchant ships could sail up the estuary as far as Helston.

Behind the bar lies 'the Loe' or 'Loe Pool', the largest freshwater lake in Cornwall and one of the many contenders to be 'the great water' into which Bedevere throws Excalibur in Tennyson's *Morte d'Arthur*. A channel has occasionally been dug across the bar to reduce the level of water in the pool when it threatened to flood parts of Helston, but the sea quickly, and mysteriously, repaired the breach.

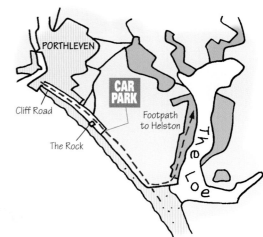

PORTHLEVEN

CAR PARK

Cliff Road

The Rock

Footpath to Helston

The Loe

Helston

Loe Bar

The stoney Loe Bar

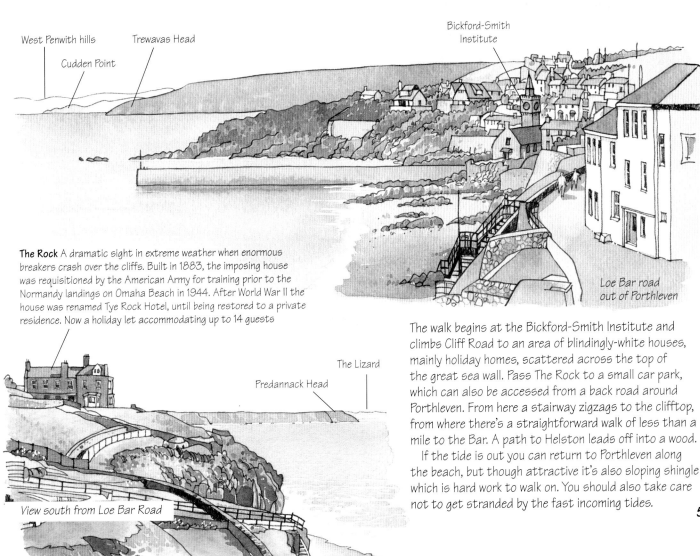

West Penwith hills

Cudden Point

Trewavas Head

Bickford-Smith Institute

The Rock A dramatic sight in extreme weather when enormous breakers crash over the cliffs. Built in 1883, the imposing house was requisitioned by the American Army for training prior to the Normandy landings on Omaha Beach in 1944. After World War II the house was renamed Tye Rock Hotel, until being restored to a private residence. Now a holiday let accommodating up to 14 guests

Loe Bar road out of Porthleven

The Lizard

Predannack Head

View south from Loe Bar Road

The walk begins at the Bickford-Smith Institute and climbs Cliff Road to an area of blindingly-white houses, mainly holiday homes, scattered across the top of the great sea wall. Pass The Rock to a small car park, which can also be accessed from a back road around Porthleven. From here a stairway zigzags to the clifftop, from where there's a straightforward walk of less than a mile to the Bar. A path to Helston leads off into a wood.

If the tide is out you can return to Porthleven along the beach, but though attractive it's also sloping shingle which is hard work to walk on. You should also take care not to get stranded by the fast incoming tides.

Narrow road through Gunwalloe, joining the A3083 at Culdrose Airfield

CAR PARK

Church of St Winwaloe

Beach café

Narrow road through Cury to join the A3083 at Trease

Golf Course

Church Cove

South West Coast Path

Poldhu Cove

CAR PARK & beach café

Mullion

Why there should be a church on this remote and storm-swept beach is unclear, but the ancient building gives a focal point for some fantastic walks along the Coastal Path. Access can be from Gunwalloe in the north or from Poldhu Cove in the south, where Marconi transmitted the world's first long-distance radio signal. Either route provides some spectacular clifftop walking.

St Winwaloe's church is one of the oldest in Cornwall. The belltower of the original 13th century building is oddly embedded in the rock of the hillside and, even more oddly, the newer 15th-century church was built some 14ft (4m) away from it.

St Winwaloe's church

CHURCH COVE

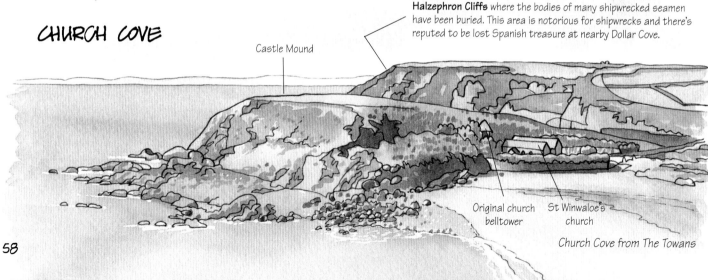

Castle Mound

Halzephron Cliffs where the bodies of many shipwrecked seamen have been buried. This area is notorious for shipwrecks and there's reputed to be lost Spanish treasure at nearby Dollar Cove.

Original church belltower

St Winwaloe's church

Church Cove from The Towans

58

MULLION COVE

Poldhu Cove

Mullion

B3296

To A3083 at Penhale

CAR PARK

B3296

MULLION COVE

Mullion is the largest village on the Lizard peninsular and within striking distance of three beaches: Poldhu; the larger but secluded Polurrian, accessible only by footpath; and dear old Mullion Cove – also known as Porthmellion – a tiny but dramatic sandy enclave with a café and an ice-cream shop.

Mullion Cove harbour

Harbour wall

There's a car park on the single access road and a gentle stroll from there down to the cove. A handful of fishing boats often bob about in a harbour as clear and blue as a municipal swimming pool. Cupped in a bowl of high cliffs, this can be a quiet and reflective place, but it's not always so tranquil. There was a lifeboat station here from 1873 to 1909, which had to deal with nine major wrecks in under a mile or so of Mullion cliffs during a period of nine years.

The National Trust owns most of the area including offshore Mullion Island, home to large colonies of breeding seabirds.

KYNANCE COVE

Residents' private vehicular access road. Also open for walkers

Beach café

Footpath to beach. Steep in places with difficult access at high tide

Albert Rock

The Bellows

Asparagus Island

KYNANCE COVE

Gull Rock

The Bishop

Sensational viewpoint

Lion Rock

CAR PARK

To A3083 Helston to Lizard road

It's often billed as a famed 'beauty spot', but calling Kynance Cove a 'beauty spot' is to seriously undersell its dramatic impact. This is nature showing off and pulling out all the stops to impress with an assortment of wildly-sculpted rock formations, white sandy beaches and an unpredictable sea with moods swinging from gentle lapping to wild fury. A National Trust car park and a clifftop viewing point provides all the facilities a visitor needs.

The Bishop

Gull Rock

The access road

But you can also venture down there, explore the nooks and crannies, caves and rock pools; walk on the beaches and paddle in the sea. A footpath winds down the cliff, steep in places with a tricky crossing of a rocky beach at the bottom, but it's well-worth the effort. There's a cafe at the bottom and a service road back to the clifftop if the footpath is covered by the tide.

The Cove is a large outcrop of serpentine, a rock unique to the Lizard that's dark and mottled with green, red and white veins.

After Prince Albert brought his children here in 1846, one of the giant rocks was named after him. I doubt that a similar honour will be bestowed on you, but after a visit here you can have the priceless privilege of remembering it for life.

The Bellows a cave that at high tide becomes a dramatic blowhole

Kynance Cliff

Asparagus Island

Albert Rock

Nantivet Rock

Café

South West Coastal Footpath

Footpath across rocky beach

Kynance Cove

61

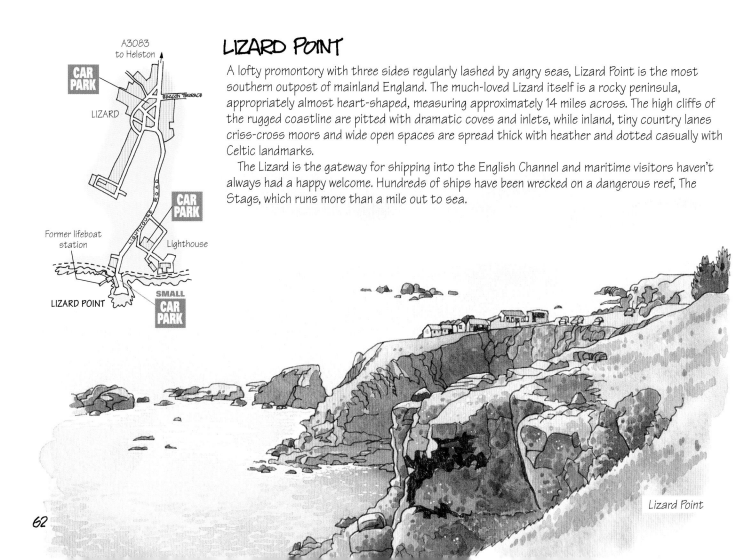

LIZARD POINT

A lofty promontory with three sides regularly lashed by angry seas, Lizard Point is the most southern outpost of mainland England. The much-loved Lizard itself is a rocky peninsula, appropriately almost heart-shaped, measuring approximately 14 miles across. The high cliffs of the rugged coastline are pitted with dramatic coves and inlets, while inland, tiny country lanes criss-cross moors and wide open spaces are spread thick with heather and dotted casually with Celtic landmarks.

The Lizard is the gateway for shipping into the English Channel and maritime visitors haven't always had a happy welcome. Hundreds of ships have been wrecked on a dangerous reef, The Stags, which runs more than a mile out to sea.

A3083
to Helston

CAR PARK

LIZARD

BEACON TERRACE

CAR PARK

LIGHTHOUSE ROAD

Former lifeboat station

Lighthouse

LIZARD POINT

SMALL CAR PARK

Lizard Point

Entrance to the Lighthouse Heritage Centre

A Lizard lighthouse has stood here in various guises since the early 17th century. The present twin-towered lighthouse, rising to 62ft (19m) tall — one tower now disused — was built in 1751 to huge protests from the locals, worried that it would throw unwanted light on their smuggling activities.

It's been automated since 1998, and is now the largest lighthouse complex in the world, once housing six keeper's families. Three enormous steam engines powered the twin foghorns, giving two blasts a minute when visibility dropped to below three miles. They still boom out every 30 seconds in foggy weather.

Former lifeboat station founded in 1859. Moved to Kilcobben Cove, near Church Cove, in 1959

The view westward from Lizard Point

The Lizard Lighthouse Heritage Centre opened in 2009 and relates the history and workings of the Lizard Lighthouse and other offshore facilities with interactive and audio-visual displays.

Unlike England's most westerly point, Land's End, which is blighted by the appalling theme park, Lizard Point has only a few long-established buildings, a couple of gift shops and a cheery little café. Most people seem to prefer it that way.

Hottentot Fig (Carpobrotus edulis) An invasive plant which has taken over many of the cliffs around Lizard Point. It's also seen in dense mats at Cape Cornwall.

Beautiful but deadly, the fig has distinctive triangular succulent leaves and large yellow flowers in early summer that fade to pink.

Introduced into gardens in the 17th century, it became a pest in the wild, destroying native plants. Listed under the Wildlife and Countryside Act of 1981, making it an offence to plant or otherwise cause this species to grow in the wild.

LIZARD WALK

With it's fresh air and open aspect, The Lizard is exhilarating walking country and taking to the splendid South West Coast Path anywhere along the coastline is as good as it gets.

This walk of around three miles begins and ends at the village green car park in Lizard. Take one of the signed footpaths out of the village to join the coastal path, then turn left and just keep walking along the grassy clifftops. Beyond Lizard Point the path narrows to pass the lighthouse. A broad downward swath takes you past the huge pit of Lion's Den, which is worth the short detour for a – very careful – look. Descend down steps to almost the waterside then climb again to the Housel Bay Hotel. A seat here is a good place to stop for refreshment and to admire the view across Housel Bay.

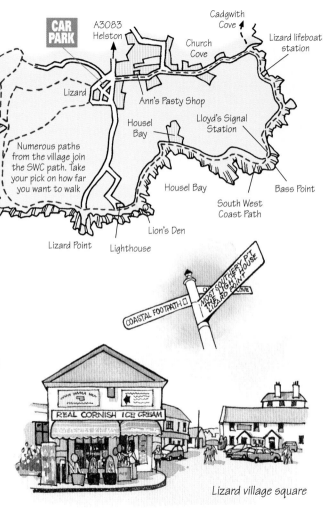

Numerous paths from the village join the SWC path. Take your pick on how far you want to walk

Church Cove thatch

Lizard village square

64

Continuing on the always clear path, you eventually arrive at the oldest surviving purpose-built wireless communications station in the world, Lloyds Signal Station. It was built to Guglielmo Marconi's instructions and the first radio signals from the Isle of Wight were received here on January 23, 1902. The station was subsequently used as a holiday home and a RAF officers' mess in World War II. It's now restored to its original 1901 condition, complete with replicas of the wireless equipment Marconi used, and is open to the public by appointment.

Ponies have been imported from Dartmoor and perform a vital role keeping down the vegetation along the clifftops.

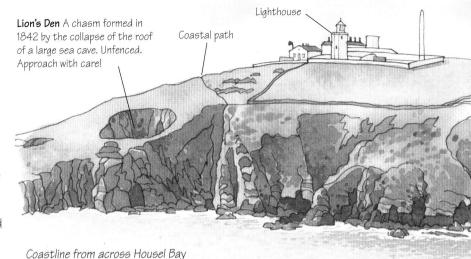

Lion's Den A chasm formed in 1842 by the collapse of the roof of a large sea cave. Unfenced. Approach with care!

Coastal path

Lighthouse

Coastline from across Housel Bay

The Signal Station and Lizard ponies

The path meanders to the lifeboat station at Kilcobben Cove – transferred from Lizard Point in 1959 – and neighbouring Church Cove, a narrow cleft in the precipitous cliffs where wire rope and winch drag crabbing boats up the stoney beach. It's now time to turn away from the sea and climb the long lane through pretty Church Cove village, but pause for a look at St Wynwallows church with its chequered tower of local granite and serpentine blocks.

When the road levels out along Beacon Terrace, it's time for another big treat to end the walk: one of Ann's Cornish pasties. They're simply the best, and endorsed by numerous celebrities including Rick Stein. You won't taste better. But note that Ann usually closes at 2.30pm and earlier if the day's pasties have sold out.

Ann's pasty shop

65

To A3083
Lizard to
Helston road

To B3293 Culdrose
Airfield to Coverack road

Ruan Minor

Footpath
into village

To A3083
Lizard to
Helston road

CAR
PARK

CADGWITH

CADGWITH

An idyllic little working village, Cadgwith has a sheltered harbour and steep streets which climb the hillsides on both sides. A small fleet of boats hauled up on the shingle beach, fish for crab, lobster and small quantities of local fish. An old pilchard cellar still stands on the quay beside the inn.

The beach is usually busy with fishermen going about their business and it's no place for visitors to lounge about getting in their way.

The village, seen from the car park path

Boats on the shingle

The harbour from The Todden

There's a fish shop in the village and a decent 17th-century pub, the Cadgwith Cove Inn. Friday nights are folk singing nights, when the Cadgwith Singers perform sea shanties in true seafaring tradition. Cadgwith also puts on a good show of Christmas lights. The fishermen prepare seafood barbecues during the summer to raise funds.

A short walk south along the Coastal footpath from the village takes you to the Devil's Frying pan, a 200ft deep collapsed sea cave; a memorable sight, especially when it's 'spitting' at high tide.

There's no public parking in the actual village. If you've been there you'll know why. It's so cramped, boats are parked along the sides of the skimpy – and only – main road. Park in the car park at the top of the village and take a beautiful footpath with some great views down to the centre. Cottages, many of them thatched, cling to the hillsides, piled almost on top of one other in a most attractive fashion.

Separating the main cove from a much smaller one is The Todden, a grass-covered outcrop of rock, topped by a classic picture-perfect thatched cottage.

The Todden

The path into the village

67

COVERACK

Unusually for a Cornish harbour village, Coverack sits exposed on a broad bay rather than being snuggled down in a sheltered cove. It's been a fishing village since AD995 with the harbour wall completed in 1724. Once the haunt of smugglers, several of the cottages are rumoured to have secret cellars for the storage of contraband.

They're hardy folks in these parts. Every Christmas Day for more than fifty years there's a been a charity swim in the bay.

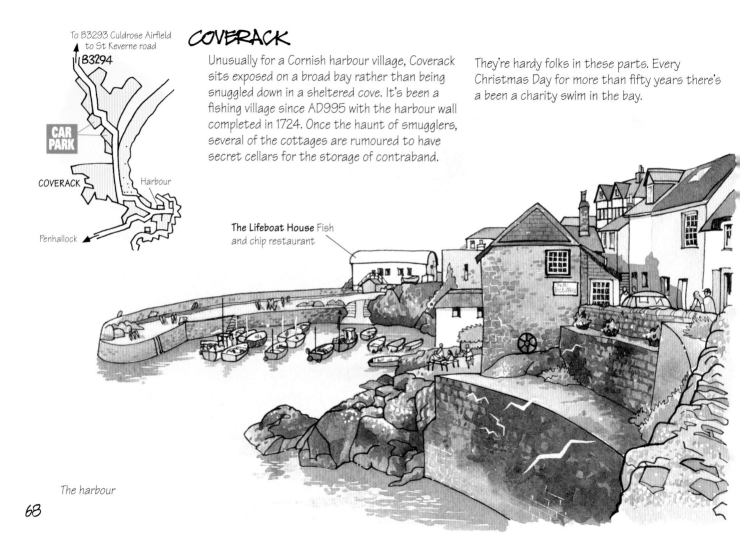

To B3293 Culdrose Airfield to St Keverne road

B3294

CAR PARK

COVERACK

Harbour

Penhallock

The Lifeboat House Fish and chip restaurant

The harbour

The harbour, looking west

Due to it's closeness to the Manacles, treacherous rocks off the Lizard, the village once had a busy RNLI station carrying out many daring launches. In 1907 the Coverack lifeboat participated in the biggest rescue in the RNLI's history, rescuing more than 500 passengers and crew from the stricken steamship SS *Suevic*. Sadly, Coverack's station closed in 1978, following the allocation of a faster boat to Falmouth, but it's now an atmospheric fish and chip restaurant, the Lifeboat House.

Despite its quiet appeal, strong community feeling and many friends, Coverack seems to have missed out on the riches that modern tourism has bestowed on the more glamorous Cornish fishing villages. Maybe that's why it has so many friends.

St Peter's church, a handsome red brick and granite building with stained-glass windows, was built in 1885 at a cost of £500 in a wonderful setting overlooking the sea.

HELFORD

Slashed across the northeast edge of the Lizard Peninsula, the Helford River has a variety of features along it's length, from a rocky mouth to sheltered muddy creeks that are well-worth exploring and, at its furthest negotiable point, the village of Gweek, internationally famous for its seal sanctuary. Frenchman's Creek is probably the most famous inlet, being the inspiration for Daphne du Maurier's novel of the same name. Close by is Helford village, a picture-perfect spot swathed in trees, which is accessible by car and a good base for riverside walks. During the summer, a passenger ferry crosses the river to Helford Passage.

There's no parking on the narrow village streets; vehicles should be left at the large car park on the outskirts where a cafe in an old chapel serves luscious crab sandwiches.

Helford from near the Shipwright's Arms

Footbridge over the stream

More thatched cottages

A riverside drink at the Shipwright's Arms

The picturesque Shipwright's Arms is a splendid riverside retreat, a smuggler's hangout in the days when these remote inlets provided a multitude of hiding places for smugglers, pirates and fugitives. There's a splendid circular walking trail to Frenchman's Creek via Penarvon Cove.

It's rumoured that every house in the village is a holiday home and the abiding feeling walking round Helford, apart from the enjoyment of it's contented attractiveness, is that you need a considerable amount of money to live here. Although there's a post office and a riverside pub, there doesn't seem to be much semblance to normal life – for the likes of me anyway.

Houses overlooking the stream

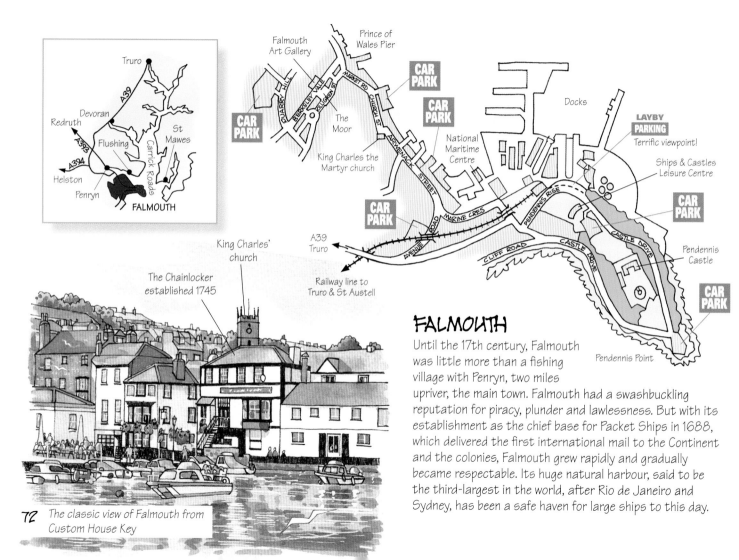

Truro

A39

Devoran

Redruth

Flushing

St Mawes

A393

A394

Carrick Roads

Helston

Penryn

FALMOUTH

Falmouth Art Gallery

Prince of Wales Pier

QUARRY HILL

BERKELEY VALE

KILLIGREW ST

MARKET RD

CHURCH ST

ARWENACK STREET

The Moor

King Charles the Martyr church

CAR PARK

CAR PARK

National Maritime Centre

Docks

LAYBY PARKING
Terrific viewpoint!

Ships & Castles Leisure Centre

PENDENNIS RISE

CAR PARK

MARINE CRES

AVENUE ROAD

CLIFF ROAD

CASTLE DRIVE

CASTLE DRIVE

Pendennis Castle

CAR PARK

Pendennis Point

CAR PARK

A39 Truro

Railway line to Truro & St Austell

King Charles' church

The Chainlocker
established 1745

FALMOUTH

Until the 17th century, Falmouth was little more than a fishing village with Penryn, two miles upriver, the main town. Falmouth had a swashbuckling reputation for piracy, plunder and lawlessness. But with its establishment as the chief base for Packet Ships in 1688, which delivered the first international mail to the Continent and the colonies, Falmouth grew rapidly and gradually became respectable. Its huge natural harbour, said to be the third-largest in the world, after Rio de Janeiro and Sydney, has been a safe haven for large ships to this day.

72 The classic view of Falmouth from Custom House Key

The granite tower of King Charles the Martyr church features on many a postcard and calendar. Falmouth was a Royalist stronghold and supporter of King Charles I who was executed by the Parliamentarians in 1649. The church was consecrated in 1665 and is defiantly dedicated to him.

Church Street

King Charles the Martyr church

Falmouth is more forward-looking than many of the more traditional Cornish holiday places. It now has a university – Cornwall's only one – established in 2008 and specialising in art, design, media and performance. There's also the National Maritime Museum, opened in 2003, the hip 'n' happening Events Square on the harbourside and, to crown all those, a Rick Stein fish and chip restaurant on Discovery Quay.

Church Street and Arwenack Street are the main shopping areas, with an eclectic mix of specialist outlets and familiar high street names, many, housed in historic buildings with maritime connections.

The Prince of Wales Pier is the bustling hub of a number of ferry and cruise boat services: across the river to affluent Flushing; the upper reaches of Carrick Roads; to St Mawes and other places along the coast.

73

The development of the docks began in 1858 with the first ship entering in 1861. The railway arrived soon after in 1863, which brought prosperity and tourism to the town. Surprisingly, Falmouth has three railway stations; Falmouth docks, Falmouth Town and Penmere. An extensive ship repair and maintenance industry continues to flourish. A layby on Pendennis Rise is a superb place to park and watch the big ships been worked on in the dry docks .

Many notable sailing achievements have begun and ended at Falmouth. Best known are Robin Knox-Johnston becoming first person to sail single-handed round the world in 1969, and Ellen Macarthur who did it in the fastest time in 2007.

During WWII Falmouth was the launching point for Operation Chariot, the famous commando raid on the heavily defended docks of St Nazaire in France, which ultimately led to the sinking of the *Bismarck* by depriving her of a repair port.

Doorway of the old De Wynn's Coffee House

Captains of Packet Ships used to gather in De Wynn's Coffee House to collect their orders. In 1702 the international mail service crossed the Atlantic to the West Indies.

The Moor is a large continental-style square, a market place and bus terminus, fringed by trees. Falmouth Art Gallery houses significant works by Gainsborough, Andy Warhol and Francis Bacon.

Falmouth Art Gallery

The Moor

Henry VIII built Pendennis Castle in 1540, at the same time as its twin on the other side of the mile-wide estuary at St Mawes, to guard the harbour entrance. One of the last Royalist strongholds to fall in the Civil War, it eventually succumbed in 1656 after a five-month siege from land and sea. It continued to be used by the military until the end of WWII and now sits rather uneasily on the same hilltop as the Ships and Castles Leisure Centre, a stark modern building overlooking the docks.

A drive around Pendennis Point is highly recommended.

Pendennis Castle

The broad stretch of water north of Falmouth docks is known as Carrick Roads, a rather odd name for a stretch of water.

Further upstream, the King Harry Ferry has traversed the River Fal at Trelissick since 1888. One of only five chain ferries in England, the King Harry carries up to 34 cars and crosses the river every twenty minutes. The alternative by road is a 27-mile detour via Truro.

Layby viewpoint

Ships & Castles
Leisure Centre

Pendennis
Castle

Falmouth Docks

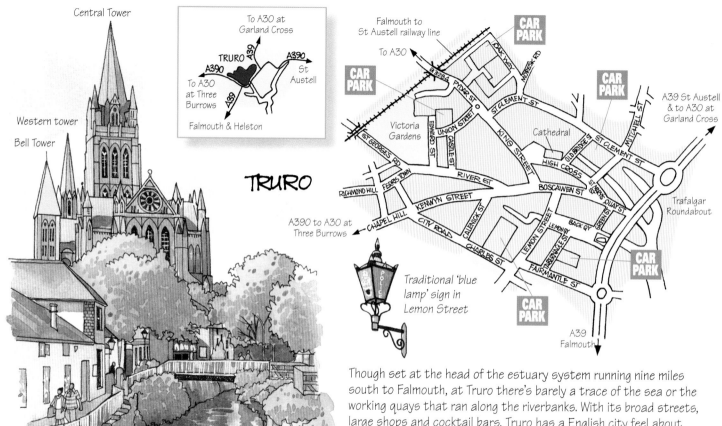

Central Tower

Western tower

Bell Tower

To A30 at
Garland Cross

TRURO

A39

A390

A390

A39

To A30
at Three
Burrows

St
Austell

A390

Falmouth & Helston

TRURO

Truro cathedral and river

Falmouth to
St Austell railway line

To A30

CAR PARK

CAR PARK

CAR PARK

A39 St Austell
& to A30 at
Garland Cross

Victoria
Gardens

ST GEORGES RD

PYDAR ST

B3284

OAK WAY

MORES RD

ST CLEMENT ST

EDWARD ST

UNION STREET

CASTLE ST

KING STREET

Cathedral

OLD BRIDGE ST

ST CLEMENT ST

MITCHELL ST

High Cross

RICHMOND HILL

FERRIS TOWN

RIVER ST

BOSCAWEN ST

ST NICHOLAS ST

ST MARYS ST

GREEN ST

QUAY ST

Trafalgar
Roundabout

A390 to A30 at
Three Burrows

CHAPEL HILL

KENWYN STREET

CITY ROAD

CALENICK ST

CHARLES ST

LEMON STREET

BACK QY

ARBANTAE ST

LEMON QY

FAIRMANTLE ST

CAR PARK

CAR PARK

A39
Falmouth

Traditional 'blue
lamp' sign in
Lemon Street

Though set at the head of the estuary system running nine miles
south to Falmouth, at Truro there's barely a trace of the sea or the
working quays that ran along the riverbanks. With its broad streets,
large shops and cocktail bars, Truro has a English city feel about
it, quite unlike the rest of Cornwall. The old quays are now a busy
outdoor area with cafe tables, markets and a variety of cultural
events. After the city centre was flooded in 1988, new flood defences
have almost completely isolated the city from its maritime past.

Boscawen Street

Coinage Hall

Cathedral

Sandwich deli

Duke Street

St Mary's Street

Central Truro

Truro has been a market town and port for more than 800 years. With cobbled streets, open squares and Georgian architecture, it's always been a well to do place where wealthy mine owners lived, preferring to keep well away from the mucky business conducted underground for them down south.

The Great Western Railway arrived in the 1860s and the start of the 20th century saw the decline of the mining industry, but by then Truro was well established as Cornwall's administration and commercial centre.

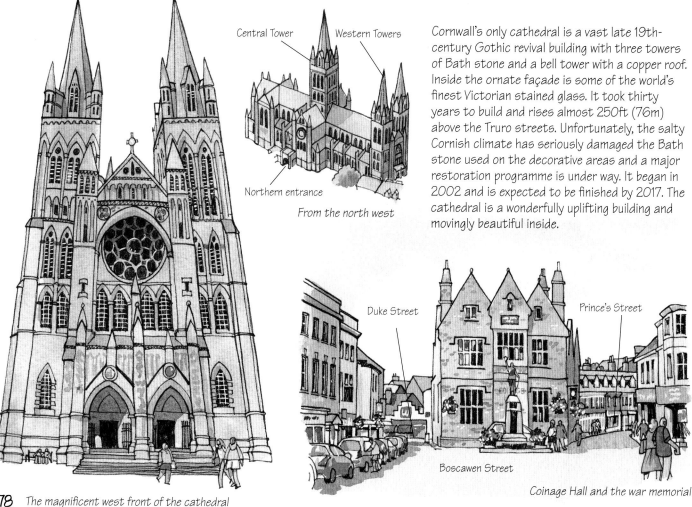

Central Tower

Western Towers

Northern entrance

From the north west

Cornwall's only cathedral is a vast late 19th-century Gothic revival building with three towers of Bath stone and a bell tower with a copper roof. Inside the ornate façade is some of the world's finest Victorian stained glass. It took thirty years to build and rises almost 250ft (76m) above the Truro streets. Unfortunately, the salty Cornish climate has seriously damaged the Bath stone used on the decorative areas and a major restoration programme is under way. It began in 2002 and is expected to be finished by 2017. The cathedral is a wonderfully uplifting building and movingly beautiful inside.

Duke Street

Prince's Street

Boscawen Street

Coinage Hall and the war memorial

The magnificent west front of the cathedral

The old Coinage Hall which stood in Boscawan Street from 1351 was the source of Truro's early wealth and status. Tin ingots were stored here before they underwent the industry's quality control test and received the Duchy stamp before being traded and shipped from the quays. The present building was built as the Cornish Bank in 1848 and is currently a tea room.

With attractive Georgian architecture, Lemon Street was built to provide easy access into Truro for the mail coaches from Falmouth, but also in honour of Sir William Lemon, member of Parliament for Cornish constituencies, 1748-1824, a total of 54 years .

Market Inn, Back Quay

Lemon Street

There are more jobs in Truro than anywhere else in Cornwall, so there's a considerable number of commuters using the roads. Driving in and out of the city can be a slow process. Avoid the morning and afternoon rush hours if you can.

If you're wondering, the river ends on the other side of the dual-carriageway A39. The rest of it is under the square.

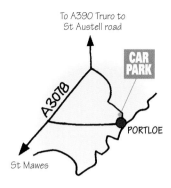

To A390 Truro to
St Austell road

A3078

CAR
PARK

PORTLOE

St Mawes

The Roseland Peninsula is an indented south-pointing tongue of land which forms the eastern margin of the Fal Estuary, or as it's usually known, Carrick Roads. The area is rich in flora and fauna, with the Perquil River splitting the southern tip, and the spidery and muddy upper reaches of the River Fal almost severing the peninsula from the mainland. It's a quietly beautiful region, largely unspoilt, of countless watery hideaways, wooded creeks, soft-sanded beaches and green hills rolling down to the sea.

PORTLOE

A remote position on the Roseland Heritage Coast; terraces of stone cottages overlooking a tiny harbour; hidden from the sea by a great outcrop of rock and a vibrant history of smuggling, especially of French brandy – Portloe is the epitome of a Cornish fishing village.

Picturesque and peaceful, it's a little gem. Park in the car park on the edge of the village, walk down the road, turn a corner and – wow! – all is revealed.

Lugger Hotel

Portloe has two inns; The Ship, at the western end, and the 17th-century Lugger Hotel which overlooks the tiny beach. You can buy a cream tea at a centre opposite the church and there's a small post office and shop. Climb the footpath on the headland opposite The Lugger for terrific views of the village and the rugged coastline.

   Inevitably, Portloe is deep in second home territory, with all the problems that brings for native Cornish people, but sadly, it's largely incomer's money which keeps places like this 'unspoilt' for voracious sightseers like me to enjoy.

The Lugger Hotel & the beach

Great footpath with steps back onto the village road

Mevagissey is another of Cornwall's ancient fishing villages and also one with a side industry which would have been of interest to the Revenue Men. These days the fishermen supplement their dwindling catches by taking visitors on fishing trips; shark for machismo adventurers and mackerel for family suppers.

The main tourist area around the harbour is a vibrant maze of twisting bottlenecks, so narrow and steep baskets of fish once had to be carried on poles between two people walking one behind the other.

The inner harbour

MEVAGISSEY

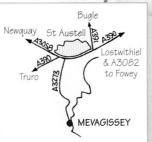

Park in a car park on Valley Road. There's an avenue of gift shops and eateries to negotiate before you reach the harbour. It's the main attraction, but narrow Church Street is also worth exploring. A walk up Polkirt Hill reveals a great view across the village to countryside on the hilltop beyond.

Mevagissey's vast harbour dates from the 1770s. Many of the stone cottages and warehouses on its northern side were built in the late 18th century, replacing original cob cottages The affluent modern housing estate on the southern hillside of Polkirt Hill caused quite a stir when it was built.

In 1895, the village became a precursor of the green revolution when a power station was built, fuelled by pilchard oil, which provided electricity for the lighthouse and surrounding streets. Local people claim that it was the first town in the country to have electric street lighting. Mevagissey also has an even greater clean credential: it was the home of Andrew Pear, the inventor of Pears Soap.

The inner harbour & Polkirt Hill

Mevagissey from Polkirt Hill

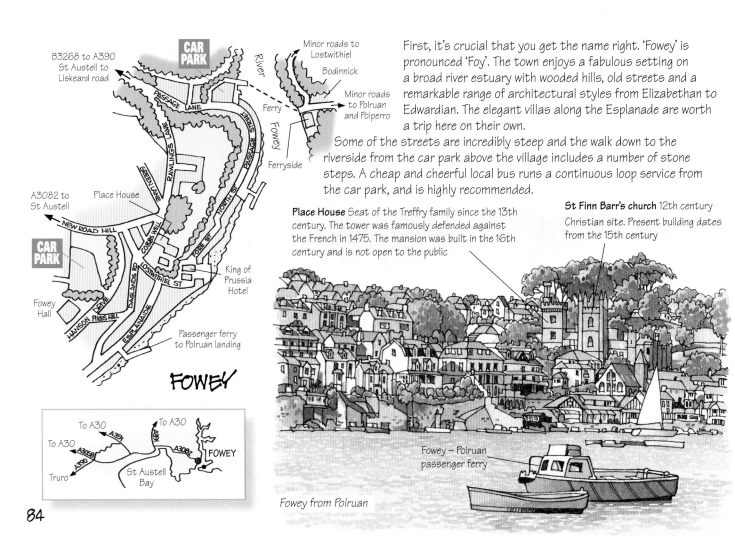

First, it's crucial that you get the name right. 'Fowey' is pronounced 'Foy'. The town enjoys a fabulous setting on a broad river estuary with wooded hills, old streets and a remarkable range of architectural styles from Elizabethan to Edwardian. The elegant villas along the Esplanade are worth a trip here on their own.

Some of the streets are incredibly steep and the walk down to the riverside from the car park above the village includes a number of stone steps. A cheap and cheerful local bus runs a continuous loop service from the car park, and is highly recommended.

Place House Seat of the Treffry family since the 13th century. The tower was famously defended against the French in 1475. The mansion was built in the 16th century and is not open to the public

St Finn Barr's church 12th century Christian site. Present building dates from the 15th century

Map labels:
- B3268 to A390 St Austell to Liskeard road
- CAR PARK
- River
- Minor roads to Lostwithiel
- Bodinnick
- Minor roads to Polruan and Polperro
- Ferry
- Fowey
- PASSAGE LANE
- RAWLINGS LANE
- PASSAGE STREET
- Ferryside
- GREEN LANE
- NORTH ST
- A3082 to St Austell
- Place House
- NEW ROAD HILL
- COZENS WELL
- FORE ST
- CAR PARK
- LOSTWITHIEL ST
- HANSON DRIVE
- DAGLANDS RD
- PIKES HILL
- ESPLANADE
- King of Prussia Hotel
- Fowey Hall
- Passenger ferry to Polruan landing
- FOWEY

Inset map:
- To A30
- To A30
- To A30
- A391
- A3058
- A390
- A3082
- FOWEY
- Truro
- St Austell Bay

Fowey – Polruan passenger ferry

Fowey from Polruan

The famous Hall Walk is a fantastic way to appreciate this area. It begins just up the steep road from the ferry landing at Bodinnick and leads around the wooded hillside to Port Creek and on to Polruan. Take the passenger ferry back to Fowey for a splendid circuit of about three miles.

The King of Prussia

Narrow streets abound

Fore Street

Built on the site of a older house and with the nickname of a notorious smuggler, The King of Prussia dates from the late 17th century.

Fore Street follows the river, passing gift shops, galleries and eventually boat yards, before arriving at the ferry at Bodinnick. It carries up to 15 cars and crosses the river every 10-15 minutes on most days of the year, saving a round trip by road of around 12 miles.

Ferryside, the Du Maurier family home, is prominent on the Bodinnick riverbank. Daphne wrote her most famous books before moving to splendid isolation at nearby Kilmarth, where she died, aged 81, in 1989.

Fowey itself also has something of the 'grand old lady' about it, but the town is no worse for that. Long may it remain so.

Polruan ferry landing

POLRUAN

Set in an ampitheatre of hills around an ancient harbour and a still busy boatyard, Polruan is almost the antithesis of sophisticated Fowey, seen so attractively across the river. There's only one access road and it's possible to drive through the streets, but the car park at the top of the town is the place to head for – and not just for parking. Cornwall has many sensational sea views but the one from the grassy hilltop across to Fowey and out to sea is exceptional. A buttress of the 8th-century St Savour's chapel shelters a pretty coastguard station nearby.

Polruan was once a major shipbuilding port and in the 19th century launched over 6,000 tons of shipping. The current boatyard, a family-run business founded in the 1920s, builds and maintains all manner of steel and wooden craft.

Walk down Battery Lane and along West Street to the harbour. Return up steep Fore Street – filled with more than 1,000 rolling balls in a unique competition during the town carnival.

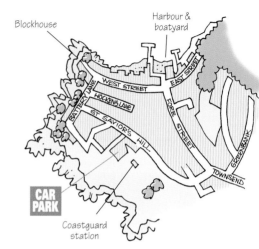

Polruan harbour & boatyard

Fowey

Fore Street

YOU MAY SIT AND REST

A thoughtful (and useful!) amenity at the top of steep Fore Street

Coastguard station

A stone blockhouse still stands on the shore, west of the harbour. There used to be a similar one on the Fowey side of the river and a chain was stretched between them for protection in times of war. The defensive device didn't always work – in 1457 a Breton fleet broke through and sacked Fowey.

Gribben Head

Readymoney Cove

Distant view of the St Austell 'Alps' (China clay waste tips)

Fowey

The view west from near the car park

POLPERRO

Don't even think of trying to drive into Polperro; it will all end in tears. Park in the large car park at the magnificently-named Crumplehorn, from where there's a pleasant walk, or a ride on a converted milk float, through an avenue of gift shops, ice cream parlours and cafes to the harbour, where the aspect opens up and you remember why you wanted to visit here in the first place.

Nestled between wooded hills, the scene of white houses and bobbing boats, familiar from a multitude of paintings, calendars and magazine images, can seem at first the ultimate Cornish fishing village cliche, prepared and preserved for the delectation of the many thousands of eager visitors.

But when they have gone, the village takes on a more personable, homely atmosphere. The evening meals — and bottles of wine — appear on the terraces, and when the sun eventually sinks into the sea the world has been amicably put to right. Of course sometimes it rains. Nowhere is that perfect.

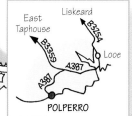

The classic view of Polperro from The Warren

In the late 18th century, Britain's wars with America and France precipitated the high taxation of many imported goods, thus boosting the smuggling trade around the Cornish coast. Spirits, tobacco and other goods were shipped from Guernsey. Polperro became the headquarters of the business, led by Zephaniah Job, a local merchant, known as 'The Smuggler's Banker'. Many wagons of contraband left here, crossing Bodmin Moor on their way to London. To combat the illegal trade, HM Customs and Excise established its first preventative station in Cornwall at Polperro, with armed officers patrolling what is now the South West Coast Path.

Ryder Lifeboat

Heritage Museum

89

A small fishing fleet still works out of Polperro, but inevitably for such a pretty place the major industry is tourism, though many of the fine houses on the hillsides were probably bought with money earned elsewhere. The Warren, which twists and turns past many a twee cottage, eventually climbs out of the main village, but there are still palatial homes on the hillside above. The question of 'How much did THAT cost?' immediately springs to mind, closely followed by 'And how did they get the furniture up there?'

South West Water recently completed a £2 billion 'Clean Sweep' programme with a £5m sewage screening station in Polperro's harbour entrance. The scheme has removed some 250 crude outfalls around the coastline and transformed the quality of bathing waters.

Bridge at the village centre

The harbour entrance

Fore Street and Landaviddy Lane are the main areas for tourist tat while Quay Road along the south side is more authentic with the quaint old Blue Peter Inn, which usually has beer kegs stacked outside. Squeeze through the gap between the cliffside and the old buildings for the main pier – a popular suntrap for day-trippers. The path beyond the pier is worth following for a look at the spectacular harbour entrance, and perhaps climb to the top of the jagged point at the end.

Enjoyment of a visit to Polperro depends on the weather and the numbers of tourists. Given a high sun and a low density of humanity, it's quite a place.

Quay Road side of the harbour

The Ryder Lifeboat

The Ryder Lifeboat is the world's only surviving Standard Self-Righting Lifeboat, now restored and on display as part of the Polperro Heritage Museum. The boat was built in 1902 and served as the Looe lifeboat until 1930, saving a total of 37 lives. Due to be broken up and burnt, the craft was saved at the last minute and restored in 1995 by C. Toms & Sons boatyard at Polruan.

ASPECTS OF CORNWALL

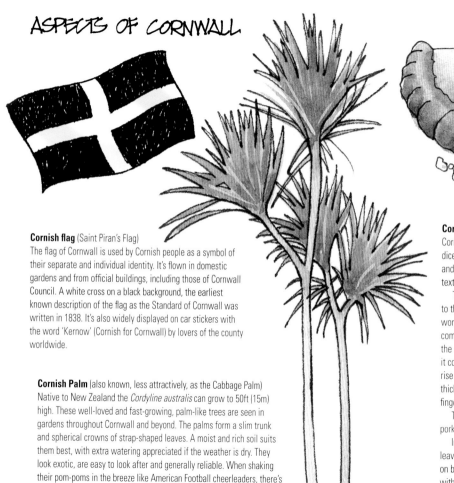

Cornish flag (Saint Piran's Flag)
The flag of Cornwall is used by Cornish people as a symbol of their separate and individual identity. It's flown in domestic gardens and from official buildings, including those of Cornwall Council. A white cross on a black background, the earliest known description of the flag as the Standard of Cornwall was written in 1838. It's also widely displayed on car stickers with the word 'Kernow' (Cornish for Cornwall) by lovers of the county worldwide.

Cornish Palm (also known, less attractively, as the Cabbage Palm)
Native to New Zealand the *Cordyline australis* can grow to 50ft (15m) high. These well-loved and fast-growing, palm-like trees are seen in gardens throughout Cornwall and beyond. The palms form a slim trunk and spherical crowns of strap-shaped leaves. A moist and rich soil suits them best, with extra watering appreciated if the weather is dry. They look exotic, are easy to look after and generally reliable. When shaking their pom-poms in the breeze like American Football cheerleaders, there's no more potent symbol of Cornwall's vitality.

Cornish Pasty The county's national dish, accounting for six per cent of the Cornish food economy. The traditional Cornish pasty is filled with beef, sliced or diced potato, swede (called turnip in Cornwall) and onion, seasoned with salt and pepper and baked. The pastry wrap can be short or a rough puff but the texture has to be firm enough to hold the filling without cracking or splitting.

The origins of the pasty are unclear, though there are many references to them throughout historical documents and fiction. It became popular with working people in Cornwall, where tin miners and others adopted it as a complete meal that could be carried easily and eaten without cutlery. In a mine the dense, folded pasty could stay warm for several hours, and if it did get cold it could easily be warmed on a shovel over a candle. Side-crimped pasties gave rise to the suggestion that the miner may have eaten the pasty holding the thick edge of pastry, which was later discarded, thereby ensuring that his dirty fingers (possibly including traces of arsenic!) didn't touch the food or his mouth.

These days pasties are made with many different fillings. In some places pork and apple are popular; there's even been a chicken tikka filling.

In Cornwall the pasty has almost spiritual status. Miners would always leave a piece of pasty in the mine for the spirits, fishermen never take pasties on board ship as they consider them bad luck at sea (and they are never filled with fish), and the Devil is said to stay out of Cornwall in case he gets baked in one.

Cream Teas

Another calorie-rich indulgence but what the heck, you're on holiday, aren't you? The standard cream tea consists of two plain, baked scones, a tub of clotted cream and a small jar of strawberry jam. It must be strawberry – any other fruit won't do.

The preparation of the ingredients is beset with as many potential *faux pas* as the Japanese tea ceremony. First the scones are carefully sliced in two and we enter the realms of controversy: Is it jam spread first with a dollop of cream on top, or the other war round? I go for the first, with jam taking preference over cream.

That sorted, is it *de rigueur* to just plonk the other buttered half on the top and bite away? Not a good idea in my experience, as the jam and cream are likely to fly out all over your best t-shirt. Keep them in halves with a dollop of jam and cream on each half. It's more manageable and you can down all the sweet stuff without looking too gluttonous.

A cup of hot tea or coffee is a suitable accompaniment. Anything in a can instantly banishes you to the ignoramus bin.

Seagulls

The seaside just wouldn't be the same without them.
The strident cry of seagulls instantly conjures up an image of the seaside.

Herring gulls are the ones most commonly seen – and heard – around the Cornish resorts. Their bright-white plumage with grey smudges and black wing tips striped with white sounds attractive enough, but their cold grey eyes, pink legs and sharply-hooked beaks with a blood-red slash indicate a darker side. They can live well into their thirties, so a life-time spent scavenging in rubbish bins and stealing visitor's chips doesn't do them much harm.

Affectionate images of the birds clog the Cornish giftshops, but up close they're scary. Look out if you're walking along the sea front with a Cornish pasty or ice cream in your hand. Gulls will steal anything they think edible and having a large seabird with a 4ft wingspan dive-bombing you while licking an ice cream is not a happy experience, especially if you're only five years old.

Ice Cream

Popular at all UK seaside places but especially in the south-west, where the air is clean and the grass is green, producing an exceedingly creamy indulgence. Available all over the county but stick to the locally-made brands for the best quality. Be careful if you're eating ice cream outside in places such as St Ives, where the seagulls have developed a vicious liking for the product.

Surfing

Dating back centuries to origins in Polynesia, surfing has a long history. Basically it's simply clinging to a piece of board on the crest of a wave while being carried towards the shore. These days, with huge commercial involvement, it's developed a multitude of variants: bodysurfing, paddle surfing, bodyboarding, longboarding, shortboarding, tow-in surfing, and wake surfing, amongst others. Predictably it has a language and culture all of its own. Surfing flourishes throughout Cornwall and supports many board manufacturers, schools and a vibrant night-life most notably at Fistral Beach, Holywell Bay, Porthleven, Whitesand Bay (Sennen Cove), Praa Sands Widemouth Bay and Whitsand Bay (near Looe).

AUTHOR'S NOTES

Arts

Since the 19th century, Cornwall, has sustained a vibrant art scene of international renown. The Newlyn School was most active at the turn of the 20th century, with leading painters Stanhope and Elizabeth Forbes, Norman Garstin and Lamorna Birch.

At the outbreak of the second world war, the painter Ben Nicholson came to live in St Ives with his then wife, the sculptor Barbara Hepworth. Together they led the St Ives School, being later

'Dual form' by Barbara Hepworth at the Guildhall, St Ives

joined by the Russian emigrant Naum Gabo and other artists including Peter Lanyon, Terry Frost, Patrick Heron, Bryan Wynter and Roger Hilton.

St Ives also houses the Leach Pottery, where Bernard Leach, and his followers championed Japanese inspired studio pottery. Modernist work still goes on in the town, with the Newlyn Society and Penwith Society of Arts still active.

Cornwall's best-known writer is probably Daphne du Maurier who lived at Menabilly near Fowey and set many of her novels in the county. Her short story, *The Birds*, turned into a memorable film by Alfred Hitchcock, must have been inspired by Cornish seagulls. Winston Graham lived at Perranporth and his famous *Poldark* series featured Cornwall heavily. David Cornwell lives and writes espionage novels in the county and is better known by his *nom de plume*, John Le Carre.

The late Poet Laureate, Sir John Betjeman was

famously fond of Cornwall and it featured prominently in his poetry. He's buried in the churchyard at St Enodoc's Church, Trebetherick. Charles Causley, the poet, was born in Launceston and is perhaps the best known of the Cornish poets.

Climate

Cornwall has a temperate Oceanic climate, the mildest and sunniest in the United Kingdom, as a result of its southerly latitude and the influence of the Gulf Stream. Winters are amongst the warmest in the country due to the southerly latitude and moderating effects of the warm ocean currents. Frost and snow are rare but summers aren't as warm as other areas of southern England. Due to its proximity to the sea, Cornwall's weather can be

St Ives fishing boat

Ferryside, the du Maurier family home at Bodinnick, near Fowey

relatively changeable. Extreme temperatures are rare, but storms and floods are common.

Economy

Largely dependent on agriculture and tourism, Cornwall is one of the poorest areas in the United Kingdom with a gross domestic product (GDP) that is just 62 per cent of the national average, and one of four UK areas that qualify for poverty-related grants from the EU. The tourist industry contributes 24 per cent of Cornwall's GDP and supports around 20 per cent of jobs.

Fishing, significantly affected by EU fishing regulations, has declined, as has agriculture, which is reliant on dairy products. The relatively poor soil of the region makes it unsuitable for growing many arable crops.

The once prosperous industry of mining (for tin, copper and rarer metals) no longer exists and several defunct mines are now World Heritage sites. The extraction of china clay continues, mainly in the St Austell district.

The Eden Centre biomes

Eden Project

A series of artificial biomes, including the world's largest greenhouse, ingeniously situated in a disued china clay pit near St Austell.

The two huge main enclosures – the Tower of London could fit into one of them – house around one million plants collected worldwide, grown in manufactured soil and maintained in constantly monitored and controlled climates. The first dome emulates a tropical environment, the second a Mediterranean.

The project took two and a half years to construct and opened to the public in March 2001.

It's an amazing place, a huge engineering, botanical and tourist-grabbing success. You really need more than one visit to take it all in. But everything is so overpoweringly 'green', sustainable and controlled – even the car parks – and oddly unnatural. The worthiness of it all can become a bit wearing. It's good to escape to a beach or a clifftop where nature is in a wild and uncontrolled state, and often a much more uplifting experience.

Geography

Cornwall forms the tip of the south-west peninsula of Great Britain exposed to the full force of the prevailing winds from the Atlantic Ocean. The coastline is composed mainly of resistant rocks that form impressive cliffs. Cornwall has a border with only one other county, Devon.

The north and south coasts have different characteristics. The north coast is on the Celtic Sea, part of the Atlantic Ocean, more exposed and therefore with a wilder nature, but there are also many stretches of fine golden sand

The south coast, dubbed the 'Cornish Riviera', is more sheltered and there are several broad

Lizard Point

estuaries offering safe anchorages. Beaches on the south coast usually consist of coarser sand and shingle, interspersed with rocky sections

The interior of the county consists of a roughly east-west spine of granite uplands, the highest land in Cornwall, which is surrounded by more fertile, mainly pastoral farmland.

Geever tin mine museum

South West Coast Path

Britain's longest waymarked, long-distance footpath and a National Trail. It stretches for 630 miles from Minehead in Somerset, along the coasts of Devon and Cornwall, to Poole Harbour in Dorset. Since it rises and falls with every river mouth, it's also one of the county's more challenging trails. The total height climbed has been calculated to be 114,931ft (35,031m), almost four times the height of Mount Everest!

In 2003, research indicated that the path generated around £300 million a year, which could support more than 7,500 jobs. The path originated as a route for the Coastguard to walk from lighthouse to lighthouse patrolling for smugglers. They needed to be able to look down into every bay and cove and as a result, the path closely hugs the coast providing excellent views, but it's rarely the most direct path between two points.

Also in the Sketchbook series...

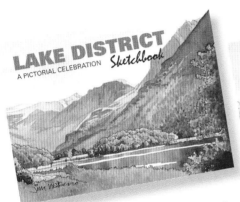

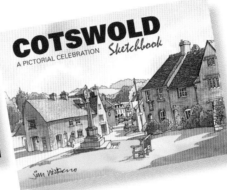

A tour of favourite Lake District towns, villages and dales, packed with colour illustrations, history, facts and figures, and some quirky surprises. The perfect guidebook, gift or souvenir.

All you need to enjoy visiting more than 35 Cotswold towns and villages. With many colour illustrations, notes on history, facts and figures, and some quirky surprises, it's the perfect guidebook, gift or souvenir.

A unique tour around the city's most famous sights, with ten easy walks from tube stations. Packed with colour illustrations, history, facts and figures, and some quirky surprises. The perfect guidebook, gift or souvenir.

Celebrating Britain's most popular tourist destinations

Survival Books • www.survivalbooks.net